Contents

Support Care

How Family Placement Can Keep
¹ldren and Families Together

Edited by
Helen Cosis Brown
Ena Fry
Joy Howard

Russell House Publishing

First published in 2005 by:
Russell House Publishing Ltd.
4 St. George's House
Uplyme Road
Lyme Regis
Dorset DT7 3LS

Tel: 01297-443948
Fax: 01297-442722
e-mail: help@russellhouse.co.uk
www.russellhouse.co.uk

ISBN: 1-903855-74-8

Typeset by TW Typesetting, Plymouth, Devon
Printed by Alden Press, Oxford

About Russell House Publishing

RHP is a group of social work, probation, education and youth and
community work practitioners and academics working in
collaboration with a professional publishing team.
Our aim is to work closely with the field to produce innovative
and valuable materials to help managers, trainers, practitioners
and students.
We are keen to receive feedback on publications and new ideas for
future projects.
For details of our other publications please visit our website or ask
us for a catalogue. Contact details are on this page.

Preface

Councils with social services responsibilities have for many years been seeking preventative services that really can offer help to families whose children are at risk of coming into the care system. The search for services that prevent family breakdown is one of the holy grails of social work.

Such services often prove elusive and local authority social services departments can struggle to run services that are accessible and are a resource to families. One reason for this is because parents in difficulties are often very fearful of an involvement with social services, believing that social workers will be seeking to remove their children if possible and not trying to help the family stay together.

The concept of 'partnership' that was intended to underpin the Children Act 1989 often seems a foreign concept to the families who are in need of services.

This background makes the development of Support Care, a truly preventive family support service, all the more inspiring. Here is a family support service that parents value, that provides real and practical help that foster carers are enthusiastically providing and that has been developed because of the belief and commitment of a few individuals.

The accounts of the social workers who developed the Support Care projects described in this book remind us that innovative, useful and respectful services can be developed by resourceful, persistent and committed staff. Each of the schemes is slightly different, but they all share a belief in the value of providing parents under stress with a series of short breaks. The foster carers who are committed to providing Support Care and who get their rewards from seeing the benefits their work brings to the children and their parents, are in no doubt that the service they provide is helping families to stay together.

The account by a parent gives insights into how Support Care can make real differences to the lives of children and families, and how it is possible to respectfully deliver services that will overcome the fears and doubts of some birth parents.

I am delighted that this book has been written and it comes at an important time. Children's services are entering a new age and are facing new challenges. The Children Act 2004 makes new demands on children's services requiring that they must be focused on delivering improved outcomes for children and young people. It is an underlying principle of the Children Act 2004 that resources must be shifted to prevention and early intervention. The intention is to provide a legislative framework that will allow local partnerships to build services around the needs of children, young people and their families. Support Care fits this agenda.

I hope that this book will be read by all those with an interest in developing practical support services that can provide a real benefit to the parents and children who require this; and I am sure that it will be of real benefit to all those who want to develop or establish local Support Care schemes.

Robert Tapsfield
Executive Director
The Fostering Network
23rd of February 2005

About the Contributors

Joanne Bell is a parent who felt greatly helped by Support Care in Bradford at a time when she was having difficulties with her son. She has been keen to share her experiences to encourage the spread of similar services elsewhere, and has travelled around the country to take part in seminars and conferences promoting the service.

Isabelle Boddy has been a qualified social worker since 1987. She began her social work career at Hull Womens Aid in 1984, where she is now Chair of the Management Committee. After eight years as a field worker and senior practitioner in Hull Social Services she has worked as Principal Practitioner, and in various management posts in District Childcare teams and Family Support teams. She is presently an Area Manager and responsible for the out-of-hours service which includes a short-break team. She is also a trainer for the Area Child Protection Committee and sits as deputy chair of Hull West Foster Panel.

Dr Helen Cosis Brown is a director of Greater London Fostering and was the Curriculum Leader for Social Work at Middlesex University from 2001–2005. She was a social worker and team leader for ten years in an Inner London social services department. She has continued to offer training in the field of fostering and adoption, and has produced a number of related publications. She currently chairs one London fostering panel and is a member of another. She sits on the Fostering Network steering group for the national Support Care project.

Pat Bugajski has been a social worker since 1984. She worked in Youth Justice until 1996 and then worked as a referral and assessment social worker. She was frustrated to witness the breakdown of families because of a lack of services available to support them during times of real crisis. She developed an interest, and became involved in, Family Group Meetings in 1999. She believes in working in true partnership with families, and was excited when Stockport decided to set up a project offering support care to families. Since 2001 she has been committed to this service as its co-ordinator.

Wanda Collins is married to Bruce and thoroughly enjoyed working as a dual registered Neighbourhood Carer and childminder for the Birmingham Neighbourhood Care Service, whilst bringing up their own four children and grandson.

Tim Earnshaw is a social worker with eighteen years experience in Children and Family Services, Child Placement and Post Adoption Support. He is a member of the North Yorkshire Adoption Panel.

Janet Exley has been a Bradford foster carer for over ten years. She was one of the first to join the Bradford Support Care Scheme seven years ago. Both she and her family have enjoyed their involvement and feel they have made a positive contribution in keeping young people at home with their own families. Janet has been happy to share her enthusiasm for her work in the presentations and seminars that have been held across the UK and hopes to continue helping to 'spread the word' over the coming years.

Ena Fry has been development worker for the Fostering Network's Young People's Project since 1990, providing information, advice and training on teenage fostering as well as working with local authorities to develop better services for young people leaving foster care. She has taken the lead within the Fostering Network on the development of Support Care. She is a member of the Department of Education and Skills' Children's Task Force and has undertaken a feasibility study on behalf of the Youth Justice Board/Home Office on the development of intensive fostering. Prior to joining the Fostering Network she worked directly with young people in a range of local authority settings including ten years developing leaving care resources in an Inner London authority.

Dr Margaret Greenfields is a Senior Lecturer in Social Policy/Sociology at Buckingham Chilterns University College. She formerly worked as a research associate attached to the Thomas Coram Research Unit. Her areas of interest include private and public family law issues, with an emphasis on parents' engagement with the legal process over matters pertaining to child protection and post-separation parenting. Margaret has a particular interest in the provision of support services to families under stress or at risk of social exclusion as a result of their 'otherness' or poverty issues. She has worked with lone-parent and same-sex families, with grandparent-carers raising children, has undertaken comparative international research into teenage pregnancy outcomes, and has extensive experience of working with gypsy and traveller communities in Britain.

Jonathan Helbert is a senior care manager with Bradford Metropolitan Borough Council's Adoption and Fostering Unit with particular responsibility for developing Adoption Support Services. Jonathan's background is as a specialist adoption social worker. He has previously worked in customer care, staff training, domiciliary services and residential childcare.

Joy Howard developed and co-ordinated Support Care in Bradford from 1996-2005. She is currently consultant to the Fostering Network and is in the process of setting up a Support Care National Network. She was a contributor to *Working with Parents* (Wheal, 2000) and *The RHP Companion to Foster Care* (Wheal, 2005).

Dr Jon Plant is currently Principal Child Care Manager with Hull City Council Social Services Department. He has worked in local authority social services for sixteen years within children's services and project-managed the development of Family Resource Centres in the city which included the development of the short break scheme. In 2002 he completed his PhD which critically examined the impact of the Children Act 1989 on children in the 'looked after' system.

Sue Smith has worked for Birmingham Local Authority for twenty-five years, initially in Education and then for Social Care and Health but always in the childcare family support field. Because of her interest in preventative work with families she jumped at the chance to set up The Neighbourhood Care Service in 1989. Initially she planned to stay for five years to get the project off the ground but after seeing the positive outcomes for families she can't think of any other post that would offer the same job satisfaction.

Dr June Statham is a Reader in Education and Family Support and a Senior Research Officer at the Thomas Coram Research Unit, Institute of Education, University of London. She has over twenty-five years experience of research into early childhood services and support for vulnerable children and their families, including children in need in the community and children who are cared for away from home, as well as informal care within families for grandchildren or older relatives. June manages the research unit's programme of 'fast response' research studies for government policy makers on issues of immediate or strategic policy relevance for the development of children's services.

Robert Tapsfield qualified as a social worker over twenty-five years ago before working, first as a generic social worker and then specialising in work with children and families. He managed a team with responsibility for children in long term-care before managing a range of children and families services. In 1999 he joined the Family Rights Group as Chief Executive and was very involved in their work promoting family group conferences, the use of kinship care and the involvement of users in planning and developing services. He became Executive Director of the Fostering Network at the beginning of 2004.

Jacqui Westwood has a background in residential childcare and youth work. She is a senior social worker in Telford and Wrekin Local Authority Family Placement Team. She was responsible for the initial design and implementation of the Part-Time Fostering Scheme in 1999. Since then she has undertaken a Post-Qualifying Child Care Award and maintains an interest in both preventative social work and supporting children with special needs.

Introduction

Helen Cosis Brown, Ena Fry and Joy Howard

The concept of offering help to families by giving parents and children or young people breaks from family tension when it threatens to become overwhelming and could end in family breakdown is not new. It is also not confined to providing resources, whether in the statutory or voluntary sectors. Family life is often difficult, and all families experience ups and downs. Most parents will acknowledge that when the going gets tough, they will call on their own parents, sisters and brothers, or friends to help out by 'having the kids' for a weekend, a few days, or an overnight to give everyone some breathing space. Families who can't call on these built-in resources can really struggle, and children can end up being accommodated by the local authority.

Public resources have been developed to help out in some circumstances; respite services for children and young people with a disability are, for example, well developed nationally. There are charitable trusts and voluntary organisations that for many years have offered holiday breaks to children and young people who are in need. However, it is only in the last decade that the concept has been applied to the wider population.

The Children Act 1989 proposed a radical new way of looking at the concept of local authority care. The renaming of Voluntary Care as Accommodation was done within the context of a new approach – partnership with parents. This was a brave new world, in which local authority care was to be a tool for helping families resolve problems rather than a removal of responsibility. Nevertheless, an episode of care, however well intentioned, was unlikely to feel any different in essence to how it had always been. Parents and their children are separated from each other, and if this happens, even for a short period, a trauma is experienced from which it is hard to recover. Moreover, if this is what is on offer in response to a family crisis, it is likely to be the resource of choice next time. It is well known that repeated episodes of accommodation lead to an almost inevitable drift to long-term care, with all the negative consequences familiar to us.

A completely new approach was needed. During the 1990s, some practitioners began to look at alternative ways of supporting families by arranging short stays away from home, with families who were approved to do this. Schemes were developed within fostering units, family support teams and childminding networks which enabled social workers, for the first time, to request a tailor-made resource for their families. The stories were all about stress, and conflict between parents and children. The underlying reasons for this varied, but all had in common the need for a low-key supportive intervention to help out during a particularly difficult time. Families didn't want to be told what to do, and wanted to remain in control of their lives. It was felt they had a right to get the help they were asking for, and this was, over and over again, just 'a break'.

There is real momentum for change at the present time, and the possibilities for development have been strengthened by the renewed government emphasis on the importance of family support, which has underpinned so much of the social policy and legislative developments of the last decade (Chapter 1). Support Care schemes are becoming more and more widely known and copied (Chapter 2). This book provides a very timely look at what Support Care is, how it works, who benefits, and why the Government is currently looking to encourage the establishment of the principles and practice of Support Care throughout the UK.

The idea for writing this book came out of the first national conference on Support Care held in 2001 (see Chapter 2). The editors wanted to collect together some of the 'stories' about the development and realisation of Support Care from the perspectives of parents, carers, practitioners, policy makers and researchers. This book is that collection. The chapters about practice, the perspectives of parents, carers and practitioners, are located between a chapter at the beginning of the book on the policy and legislative context of Support Care and a chapter at the end of the book about a research study on Support Care. This last research chapter is the concluding chapter as it brings together and synthesises the themes that are illuminated throughout the practice chapters. By definition the styles of the chapters vary both in length and in degrees of the formality of presentation. We have seen this as one of the strengths of the book rather than a detraction.

Support Care is not a uniform provision, as will be seen throughout the book. Each chapter details the individuality of each of the Support Care schemes. Because of that individuality even the terminology differs which ranges from Support Care to Neighbourhood Care, to Part-time Fostering to Short Breaks. We were able to gather together five local authorities' experiences of developing and running Support Care schemes with the support and permission of their Social Services Directorates. These included: Bradford; Birmingham; Stockport; Telford and Wrekin, and Hull. Some chapters draw on case studies to illuminate the detail of the schemes. In all these case studies all names and identifiable details have been changed to ensure anonymity.

We start the book with a contextualising chapter (Chapter 1) by Ena Fry from the Fostering Network. This chapter makes links between different legislative and policy developments from the Seebohm Report onwards right through to current social policy focusing on family support and prevention. She locates Support Care firmly within the context of the Government's current children and families agenda. This chapter also details the Fostering Network's current role in collating and disseminating best practice in this area as part of its Support Care national project funded by the Department of Education and Skills.

Chapters 2, 3, 4 and 5 are all from Bradford and are approached from the perspectives of: the Support Care Co-ordinator; a parent; a carer and three practitioners involved with adoption support. Joy Howard's chapter (Chapter 2) describes the long and committed struggle not only to develop Support Care in Bradford but also to disseminate the ideas nationally. This chapter develops the theme of working in 'real' rather then 'rhetorical' partnership with parents; a theme echoed in the following chapters. The chapter, as well as being a record of the grassroots development of this Support Care scheme, also relates the work that was involved in putting Support Care onto the national agenda. This chapter is followed by Joanne Bell's account (Chapter 3) of her and her son's experience of using Support Care. This chapter illustrates the importance, as a parent, of being able to receive help but at the same time to be enabled to feel and to remain in control. Janet Exley's chapter (Chapter 4) is written from her years of experience as a carer, offering Support Care to children, young people and families. Her chapter also reflects Joanne Bell's theme of enabling parents to stay in control of their own and their children's lives. She describes how Support Care can provide a 'lifeline' at a difficult time for a family and as a result prevent a family breakdown, which might result in children being separated from their families. Her chapter brings to life the richness of working with both children and their parents, and balancing the tensions as well as the benefits this places on the carer's own children.

Joy Howard, Jonathan Helbert and Tim Earnshaw write the last of the Bradford collection (Chapter 5). Each practitioner writes from their own perspective, in relation to a piece of work they undertook where Support Care was used to retain an adopted child within their adoptive family. This chapter demonstrates how Support Care can be effectively utilised as part of an adoption support package. The authors also are able to show how Support Care for adoptive families should not be seen as a simple replication of how Support Care might be used with families with their own birth children. There are inevitably different dynamics at play between all the individuals involved and these need to be taken into account in designing Support Care packages for adoptive families. The chapter also raises an ethical question in relation to support to adoptive families. How do we resolve the dilemma of offering resources to adoptive families to help their adopted children remain with them, when in many cases those children's own birth families may well have been offered no such preventative resource themselves?

Chapter 6, written by Sue Smith, describes the Birmingham Neighbourhood Care Scheme, which was developed originally within their childminding provision and to where it has recently returned. This chapter elaborates upon some of the practical difficulties faced by local authorities, relating to legal and policy matters, when setting up and running Support Care schemes. Similar issues are highlighted by Ena Fry's chapter (Chapter 1) setting out the policy and legislative context of Support Care. Sue Smith emphasises the importance of 'locality' in preventative work for children, families and carers. She examines the role of Support Care in tackling social exclusion for families, who for whatever reason feel themselves to be on the 'outside' or on the 'edge'. She draws on data from ongoing evaluation of the Scheme to give voices to all parties' views that Support Care is an effective preventative resource.

Sue Smith's chapter is complemented by that of a Birmingham carer from the Neighbourhood Care Scheme, Wanda Collins (Chapter 7). Wanda Collins' and Janet Exley's chapters, both written from the perspective of carers, show how Support Care can be a vehicle to retain experienced carers, as well as attract new carers, to a provision which is flexible and does not have to be full time. Wanda Collins' chapter re-visits Sue Smith's theme of 'locality' emphasising through the use of case study examples the importance of 'neighbourhood' for children and families. She also demonstrates the importance of continuity for both children and parents and how local preventative provision enables this to evolve in a natural fashion. Both carers' chapters refer to Support Care being a 'lifeline' for families. These are the people working at the coalface of prevention and their assessment of the importance of Support Care as a preventative intervention should not be underestimated.

Pat Bugajski (Chapter 8) draws on a number of case studies from the Stockport Short Breaks scheme where she is the Co-ordinator. These case studies speak for themselves and evidence the role Support Care can have in reversing a seemingly dire prognosis for children and families who have already been subject to statutory intervention. Here case studies are a testament to the intimate working relationships between, carer, parent and child and how real prevention or reversal of a difficult set of circumstances can only happen when the people involved are committed to open, warm and clear relationships which are underpinned by integrity. The chapter shows how Support Care can be used effectively as a 'stitch in time'.

Jacqui Westwood (Chapter 9) builds on the theme of relationships focusing her chapter on attachment. By drawing on evaluative research undertaken by her as the Senior Social Worker responsible for the Telford and Wrekin's Part-time Fostering scheme she discusses the strengths as well as the tensions involved. She locates Support Care firmly at the centre of work with children and families as an effective way of sustaining children within their own families and preventing them drifting into 'care'. By drawing on a number of case studies she is able to demonstrate how Support Care enables children to maintain their primary attachments. She also offers a useful discussion about the legal and policy context of Support Care and how Telford and Wrekin's scheme has navigated this labyrinth.

Isabelle Boddy and Jon Plant (Chapter 10) describe Hull's Short Break scheme. This chapter illustrates some of the differences between the different local authority Support Care schemes described in this book and their inceptions. The Hull scheme is the only one that was established as part of a Social Services Directorate's initiative in the late 1990s to re-focus on preventative work with children and families. However, the Hull scheme shares, in common with some of the other local authorities, its history of being relocated – endemic in local authority reorganisations. The chapter details the history of the scheme. They sum up much of the ethos of all the schemes within the book when they write that their Short Breaks Support Care scheme 'aimed to place family support at the heart of all our interventions. Short breaks were therefore to be presented as offering a positive opportunity, rather than the orthodox perception of accommodation as a second-best option, or a last resort'.

The last chapter, written by June Statham and Margaret Greenfields from the Institute of Education, gives an overview of their research, which examines Support Care schemes in the UK, and tells us what is known to date and what is yet to be established. The authors draw on findings from their research, which was undertaken as part of the Government's Choice Protects review. The study looked at the barriers preventing local authorities setting up Support Care schemes and how those barriers might be overcome. This chapter provides some of the main findings of the study. Interestingly, but not surprisingly, some themes identified from their study closely reflect the content of the chapters in this book, those being: parents being in control; help in a crisis; flexible response; current ambiguity in relation to schemes' legislative positions; prevention is better than cure; as well as many others.

In summary, the book offers a detailed tour of Support Care and evidences how it can be central to preventative work with children and families. It also shows how foster carers can be utilised as part of a preventative strategy. Carers, rather than becoming an 'alternative family' or the 'substitute family' for a child are working with parents to help them cope in times of crisis or difficulty to enable them to remain in control of their own and their children's lives. By doing this carers are being used in creative, flexible ways to support other families and their children.

There are a number of differences between the Support Care schemes within the book including: terminology; location of the provision within the local authority structure; whether the scheme was developed from a directorate or a grassroots initiative and how the different schemes have navigated policy and legislative ambiguities. However, there are many more common themes that emerge including: the commitment and tenacity of those involved in establishing the provision; the emphasis on prevention; real respect for both children and parents; close working relationships between carers, children and parents; flexibility; and, lastly, a needs-led perspective. But, what is probably the most striking theme that emerges from the chapters is the fundamental belief that if you work *with* parents in a 'respectful' and 'facilitative' manner you are more likely to engage them and so facilitate the changes that might be needed to enable them to remain as active parents and prevent their children going into care.

The overuse of such words and terms as 'respect', partnership', 'working together' within the discourses of social policy and social work has meant that they can ring hollow. The word that comes through most powerfully in this collection and isn't 'hollow' but is however a word which is not fashionable in social work is 'kindness'. The carers and the social workers were experienced as 'kind' and that was probably one of the most important factors that contributed to the positive outcomes. We end the introduction with words from a parent, Nighat, a young mother with five children, (Chapter 6) who sums this up better than we can. She and her children are the most important players within Support Care along with other parents and children she represents.

I was a little bit scared of leaving my children and what would be thought of me but everyone was so nice and they know so much about what children need and they were kind to me.

Chapter 1

Support Care: The Wider Context

Ena Fry

Introduction

The Seebohm Report recommended 'a new local authority department providing a community based and family orientated service, which will be available to all' (Seebohm, 1968: 11).

In his lecture entitled *Seebohm, The Green Paper and Future Hopes*, Lord Laming said:

> *Seebohm saw social services as being an outward looking proactive organisation that would engage with the community, that would be seen as a positive force in local communities, tackling exclusion, poverty and promoting the well being of the community. The Victoria Climbié Enquiry, in contrast had evidence of an entirely reactive approach by all of the services.*
>
> (Laming, 2003)

How have we moved from a position of vision and hope to one of reaction and blame? How can a national organisation like the Fostering Network with a specialist focus help childcare services move forward in the spirit of Seebohm? What contribution can the development of Support Care services make?

As the project development worker for the Fostering Network's Support Care Project, in this chapter I will consider:

- The legislative and policy framework that underpins Support Care.
- The Fostering Network's role as a non-government organisation in the development and promotion of Support Care services nationally.

Support Care is the preventative face of foster care. It aims to provide a part-time fostering service. The task differs from that normally undertaken by foster carers in that a placement is offered before, rather than after a situation has reached the point of breakdown. As a service it sits at the interface between family support services and fostering. Support Care is adaptable so

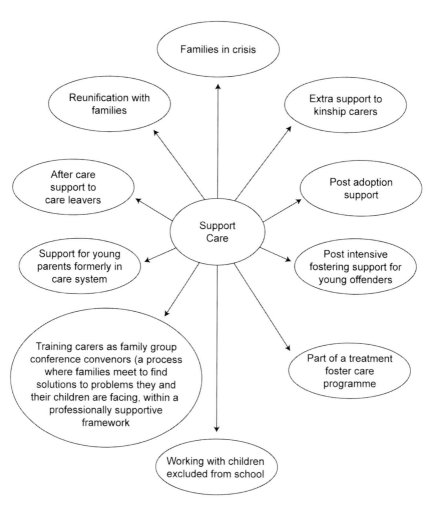

Figure 1.1   Varied uses of Support Care

can be applied to a range of other services to strengthen and support the care given by parents and carers as shown in the diagram above.

The legislative background to Support Care

The Children Act 1989 set a preventative agenda in line with Seebohm, but during the 1990s it was severely eroded because of the concentration of increasingly scarce resources on child protection. This was partly reflective of the failure to provide sufficient funding to implement The Children Act 1989 fully in the first instance. This preoccupation with child protection has resulted in services being primarily organised around *crisis* so the response by social services and other relevant departments often happens after the damage has been done.

Since the Labour Government came into power in 1997, the pendulum has begun to swing back towards prevention and social inclusion through better identification of need and working with parents to prevent admission into the public care system. The Green Paper *Every Child Matters* states:

When we consulted children and young people and their families, they wanted the Government to set out a positive vision of what, as a society, we want to achieve for our children. They wanted an approach that was less about intervening at a point of crisis or failure and more about helping every child to achieve his or her potential. They wanted an approach that involved children, families, communities and public services working together to a shared set of goals, rather than to narrow and contradictory objectives.

(HM Treasury, 2003a: 6)

The resultant Children Act 2004 has provided an opportunity for every local authority to:

- Do a thorough assessment of the needs of children and young people and their families in their area.
- Draw together varied means by which it is possible to work with the community in harnessing new ways of supporting children and families.

Support Care services are ideally placed to make a significant contribution to achieving the objectives set out in the Green Paper and the Children Act 2004.

Table 1.1 sets out the key legislation and guidance that impact on Support Care services.

So the Government's emphasis is on:

- *Supporting parents and carers* who are at the heart of improving children's lives. This is to be achieved through universal services such as: support programmes for fathers as well as mothers; and targeted and specialist support such as the extension of the Sure Start home visiting service; parent education programmes and family group conferencing.
- *Better prevention* through: the integration of education, health and social care around the needs of children; extended Children and Adolescent Mental Health Services (CAMHS); improved youth services; tackling anti-social behaviour and bullying.
- *Earlier intervention* will be achieved through: clearer accountability; integrated service provision; and workforce reform.

Significant government funding to support developments to achieve these aims includes:

Table 1.1 Government legislation and guidance relating to Support Care

Year	Legislation guidance	Key/relevant principles in relation to Support Care
1989	*The Children Act*	Key principles: • The best place for children to be looked after is within their own family • the parents should be involved in planning their child's future and legal proceedings should be unnecessary • the welfare of children should be promoted by a partnership between the family and the local authority • the child's needs arising from race, culture, religion and language must be taken into account.
1989	*UN Convention on the Rights of the Child* (UN, 1989)	Article 9 states: 'parties shall ensure that a child shall not be separated from his or her parents, against their wishes except when competent authorities determine that such separation is necessary for the best interest of the child'.
1998	*Modernising Social Services* (DoH, 1998a)	The central theme was that everyone benefits if social services are providing good, effective services to those who need support. The aims were to be delivered within the Quality Protects Programme.
1998	*The Quality Protects Programme* (DoH, 1998b)	The Quality Protects Programme was a key part of the Government's wider strategy for tackling social exclusion. It focused on working with some of the most disadvantaged and vulnerable children including those in the Child Protection system and others. The programme ended in 2004.
1999	*The UK National Standards for Foster Care* (NFCA, 1999a)	Twenty-five standards defining the specific needs of children and setting out the rights of each child or young person in foster care. How effective and appropriate care is provided by each foster carer; and how each local authority can offer a high quality foster care service for all who can benefit from it.

1999	*The Code of Practice on the Recruitment, Assessment, Approval, Training, Management and Support of Foster Carers* (NFCA, 1999b)	Provided for a more rigorous assessment of prospective carers taking account of the vulnerability of children and young people needing foster care. This needs to inform the recruitment and assessment of households approved to provide Support Care placements.
1999	*Working Together to Safeguard Children* (DoH, HO and DfES, 1999)	Sets out how all agencies and professionals should work together to promote children's welfare and how actions to safeguard children fit within the wider context of support to children and families.
2000	*Framework for the Assessment of Children in Need and their Families* (DoH, 2000)	Jointly issued by Department of Health, Department of Education and Employment and Home Office. The aim of this practice guidance is to make transparent the evidence base for the Assessment Framework, thereby assisting professionals in their tasks of analysis, judgement and decision-making with regard to children in need and their families.
2000	*The Care Standards Act*	Part I provides for the establishment of the National Care Standards Commission in England and the National Assembly for Wales as the equivalent authority in Wales. Part III makes provision for the inspection of local authority fostering and adoption services by the National Care Standards Commission (amalgamated with the Social Services Inspectorate to form the Commission for Social Care Inspection in 2004). Part V provides the regulation of childminding and daycare services for younger children and provides checks on the suitability of persons working with older children.
2001	*Ofsted Regulations* (DfES, 2001)	Permits childminders to become registered to provide overnight care for up to 27 days.
2001	Connexions	Brought together the work of six government departments together with youth and careers services to support young people aged thirteen to nineteen. The aim is to provide integrated advice, guidance and access to education, training and employment opportunities.

Table 1.1 *Continued*

Year	Legislation guidance	Key/relevant principles in relation to Support Care
2002	*Fostering Regulations and Guidance* (DoH, 2002a)	Provides a comprehensive compulsory code for all fostering services.
2002	*National Minimum Standards for Fostering Services* (DoH, 2002a)	Thirty-two national standards that form the basis of the regulatory framework for all fostering agencies under The Care Standards Act 2000.
2002	*Choice Protects Programme* (DoH, 2002b)	The Government's three-year review of fostering and placement services. Launched in March 2002 to improve outcomes for looked after children through providing better placement stability, matching and choice. Specific reference to Support Care as part of local authorities having a full range of placement options to meet local needs.
2002	*Fostering for the Future: an SSI Inspection report* (DoH, 2002c)	This report identified: • a poor understanding of the costs of providing foster care • lack of information and benefits of in-house services compared to those provided by Independent Fostering Providers • difficulties with recruitment and retention of foster carers.
2002	The Adoption and Children Act s116: *Local Authority Circular 13* (DoH, 2003a)	Some local authority lawyers have argued that these two amendments to Section 17 of the Children Act 1989 means Support Care placements can be provided under Section 17 as opposed to Section 20. The Adoption and Children Act also provides entitlement to assessment of needs post-adoption and the possible option of a post-adoption support package.
2003	Green Paper *Every Child Matters* (HM Treasury, 2003a)	The Government's stated intention is to put supporting parents and carers at the heart of its approach to improving children's lives as families and carers are the most critical

influence on children's lives. The policies and proposals set out in the Green Paper *Every Child Matters* were designed to protect children and maximise their potential. Setting out a framework for services that cover children and young people in England from birth to 19, it aims to reduce the number of children who experience educational failure, engage in offending or anti social behaviour, suffer from ill health, become teenage parents or victims of abuse and neglect.

2004 The Children Act

Central to this Act is the aim to achieve the following five key outcomes for all children:

• being healthy
• staying safe
• enjoying and achieving
• making a positive contribution
• economic well being.

2004 Regulations for independent reviewing officers (IRO) (DfES, 2004)

The Government is updating the Review of Children's Cases Regulations 1991 and has introduced the role of IRO on a statutory basis. The new regulations will require all IROs to:

• chair the reviews of all looked after children
• be responsible for monitoring the local authority's work on the care plan, with the aim of minimising 'drift' and challenging poor practice
• refer a case to the Children and Family Court Advisory and Support Service (CAFCASS) to take legal action as a last resort.

2005 Integrated Children's System (www.doh.gov.uk/ integratedchildrenssystem) (DfES, 2003)

A conceptual framework to lead work with children and families in need. System comprises three main elements:

• a framework for assessment, planning, intervention and reviewing
• core date required setting out essential information for effective practice with children and families and for planning services
• exemplars.

- *Children's Fund* to provide support services for children aged five to thirteen (Twenty-five million pounds) (HM Treasury, 2003b).
- *Sure Start funding.* The Sure Start Programme is the cornerstone of the Government's drive to tackle child poverty and social exclusion. It aims to achieve better outcomes for children and families by increasing daycare for all children under four, and supporting parents. Launched in 1998, currently in England there are approximately five hundred and twenty local partnership schemes. The budget for 2005–6 is one and a half billion pounds with an additional six hundred and sixty-nine million pounds by 2007–8 (www.surestart.gov.uk/aboutsurestart/)
- *Children and Mental Health Services grant.* Three year funding of one hundred and forty million pounds to local CAMHS via local authorities to build capacity, improve access and help to deliver a comprehensive mental health service for children and young people (DoH, 2003b).
- *The Parenting Fund.* In the 2002 Spending Review the Government announced a twenty-five million pound grant for voluntary and community organisations to develop services that would enable parents and families to: *Access the support, help and advice they need to expand support available to parents. Increase support services for groups who currently receive little access e.g. black and ethnic minority communities.*

(HM Treasury, 2003b)

Future developments that will impact on Support Care

- Children's Trusts.
- Treatment foster care and intensive fostering.

Children's Trusts

The establishment of Children's Trusts as set out in the Green Paper *Every Child Matters* (HM Treasury, 2003a) and the resultant legislation, The Children Act 2004 will provide opportunities to deliver integrated services which are more accessible to users through joining up education, social care and health services. This will build on and develop work already happening at local level through organisations such as Connexions, Sure Start and other Early Years initiatives. There is no single model but all will be developed within the context of the long term vision within the Children Act. Children and young people and their families are at the heart of service design and delivery.

Treatment foster care and intensive fostering

Treatment Foster Care is currently being piloted by the Department for Education and Skills in selected local authorities. Targeted at young people aged ten to sixteen, who are displaying severe levels of challenging behaviour or self-harming,and who are likely to have experienced a number of placement changes. This service is based primarily on work undertaken in Oregon. The programme is based on a wrap-around service that includes CAMHS, Health and Education Services and Councils with Social Service Responsibilities (CSSR) (DoH/DfES, 2004).

From October 2004, courts were able to include a fostering requirement as part of a Supervision Order (The Anti-Social Behaviour Act 2004, Section 88, Schedule 2). Intensive fostering is shortly to be piloted by the Youth Justice Board, and again will be based on a service that wraps around the young person and their family.

In both instances, there is scope for using Support Care whether to support a fostering placement or facilitate successful reunification with the young peoples' own families by the provision of post-placement support.

The Fostering Network's role in the development and promotion of Support Care

The vision set out in the Green Paper *Every Child Matters* (HM Treasury, 2003a) and enacted in the Children Act 2004, endorsed earlier principles in the Children Act 1989 and requires a huge shift from the emphasis on protection, to prevention. It means moving services from being reactive to being proactive and engaging with children and young people and their families. Support Care is ideally placed to address this approach and objectives but needs to become mainstream in every local authority rather than an optional extra in some. That is where the Fostering Network has a unique role to play.

As a national membership organisation with nearly all local authorities in membership, the Fostering Network can access key people at local level who either have a policy or strategic role or are managers and workers with responsibility for managing and delivering effective practice.

The Fostering Network seeks to promote the best interests of children and young people in foster care by the following:

- Provision of information.
- Sharing and promotion of good practice.
- Use of its varied membership to inform, influence and contribute to developments both at government and local levels.

The Fostering Network is taking the lead in addressing key issues facing foster care services at the beginning of the 21st century including:

- The shortage of families coming forward to foster.
- The retention of experienced foster families.
- Listening and responding to the views and experiences of children and young people and their families.

- Reducing placement moves.
- Better matching particularly in relation to children and young people of dual heritage.
- Valuing and improving the status of foster carers.
- The provision of improved training for all involved in the fostering service.

Support Care is the preventative face of foster care, taking us back to the core principle in the Children Act 1989 which is that wherever possible children and young people should be supported to remain within their own families. At a time when the emphasis has been increasingly on adoption (Adoption Act 2002) its development is necessary to provide a balance to thinking and planning comprehensive holistic child care services in line with recent legislation and guidance.

The essence of Support Care is the provision of a non-stigmatising service, which is a key objective of the Fostering Network's five-year plan. The Fostering Network's commitment to Support Care has its origins in two separate but significant roots:

- The views and wishes of children and young people in foster care as outlined below.
- An approach from a membership local authority with a Support Care service.

The publication in 1999 of the *UK National Standards for Foster Care* (NFCA, 1999) was the outcome of the most comprehensive consultation exercise ever undertaken on the quality of foster care services. The publication set out how each local authority could offer a high quality fostering service for all who could benefit from it. A significant contribution to the content and shaping of these standards was provided by over a thousand children and young people who, through questionnaires and group meetings provided valuable information, insight and ideas on the future shape of foster care. As the development worker for the Fostering Network Young People's Project, I took the lead on this consultation process with a care-experienced young person. The most significant finding was that, however good their experience of living in a foster home, for the majority what they really wanted was to be back home in their own families. Foster-family training days and other consultation events delivered the same message.

So how could we meet this simple but complex request? What was the challenge that faced the Fostering Network and the Young People's Project in particular? Within months of the publication of the *UK National Standards for Foster Care* (NFCA, 1999a) out of the blue came a phone call from Joy Howard in Bradford (see Chapter 2). She felt passionately that Support Care had a future not just in Bradford but throughout the UK and who better to promote it than the Fostering Network? It was another challenge, and the beginning of a fruitful partnership that still has far to go but has already proven to be an effective answer to children and young people's wish to be within their own families.

Since 2000, the Fostering Network, together with Bradford's Support Care scheme and, from 2001, Birmingham's Neighbourhood Support Care scheme (see Chapter 6), all have worked together to promote the development of Support Care. A two-year grant from Lloyds TSB in 2001 enabled us to undertake a series of regional seminars (road shows). These were well received. Whether considering establishing a Support Care scheme or improving an existing service, everyone welcomed the opportunity to meet, share and highlight good practice and issues of concern. It was an energising, exciting and valuable experience for us as organisers. As Bradford's Joy Howard often said, 'with Support Care there are no losers'. So, at a time of severe staff shortages, reduced budgets, increased costs of family placements and increasing demands on social care services generally, Support Care with its effective outcomes and value for money was a welcome option. However, it was, and to some extent still is, like a little tug trying to turn a liner, which is set on a fixed course. The local authorities who came on board never doubted its potential but in others we began to understand a sea change would be needed in attitude as well as in the use of resources.

Unlike so many aspects of the care system, the regional road shows were truly collaborative; demonstrating that partnership with parents can be a reality. The team included two Support Care providers, one dealing with mainly under eights and the other mainly older children and a parent who was and is a staunch champion of Support Care. Indeed, her ending statement at each presentation was 'if you haven't got a Support Care scheme, why not?' A challenge indeed!

If we needed proof that we were on the right track then the regional events proved it. Also, the team was invited to be the guest speakers at the annual Fostering Network conference in Northern Ireland. Again the enthusiasm and response was overwhelming, with an excellent full-spread feature in the Irish News. No wonder we felt confident to take the message about Support Care to the Association for the Directors of Social Services (ADSS) conference in 2003 where forty-five directors and equivalent decision-makers joined us.

The ending of the Lloyds TSB funding coincided with the publication of the Green Paper (HM Treasury, 2003a) with its focus on the development of family support services. So, the time was right to apply for funding to further develop Support Care nationally.

The awarding to the Fostering Network of a three-year Safeguarding Children and Supporting Families Project grant by the Department for Education and Skills in April 2004 made extending the work possible. Two part-time workers have been appointed to undertake the following work and address the following issues:

- Assist nine local authorities to develop Support Care schemes.
- Evaluate the effectiveness of Support Care as a mainstream service for children and young people and their families.
- Provide accessible, detailed information that can be disseminated to other authorities seeking to set up Support Care services.
- Contribute to the retention of foster carers who can no longer foster full-time.
- Support the recruitment of new carers who are unable to commit to being full-time foster carers.
- Establish a database of relevant contacts and resources as the basis for a national Support Care network.
- Assist local authorities to meet new government objectives relating to children in need including supporting parents and carers, early intervention and effective protection.
- To establish contacts with relevant government departments and other bodies, e.g. the ADSS to highlight difficulties for Support Care schemes and to work on solutions.
- To make presentations, write articles, arrange press releases on Support Care to inform interested organisations or bodies.
- To develop and take responsibility for servicing regional Support Care forums for the exchange of information and practice development
- To plan and deliver a national conference on Support Care and the findings of the project in year three.

Key areas for future consideration

Legal status of children and young people placed in Support Care

A major factor facing Support Care is the need to clarify the legal status of children and young people. An overnight stay with a foster carer constitutes a period of accommodation, i.e. under Section 20. However, Support Care placements are often only monthly for one night so the looked after children paperwork and system can be onerous. Currently, most existing Support Care services make placements on the basis of Section 20, often using simplified Looked after Children paperwork. Since November 2003 Birmingham have placed children under Section 17 (6). Their carers have always been dual-registered i.e. as foster carers and childminders. Ofsted's childminding standards (DfES, 2003b) appeared to Birmingham's legal advisors to be sufficiently comprehensive to protect each child in placement provided additional safeguards are in place (See Chapter 6). The danger is that other agencies could set up schemes under section 17 (6) without such safeguards. Support Care requires fully trained and well-supported carers to undertake skilled work with children and young people 'in need' and their parents. It is never a scheme that is just an agreement between a parent and a minder.

Clearly, a system needs to be in place that applies to all Support Care services; one that fully safeguards children but doesn't stigmatise families, with paperwork that is not cumbersome but appropriately meets the needs of the service. It is essential that decisions are reached and become part of the proposed Integrated Children's System.

Better guidance and clarification may serve to encourage more authorities to develop Support Care services. This is an issue on which the Fostering Network can take a lead, to consult with relevant government departments.

Recording Support Care statistics

Currently, recording children and young people in Support Care as looked after children does have an adverse effect on indicators of placement stability and looked after children indicators. Currently, if a child is placed on six occasions with the same Support Carer as part of an agreed plan it could be recorded as six admissions or placements. If new guidance were introduced so Support Care placements were given a separate recording this would provide a more realistic picture.

Review arrangements

Again, clarification of the previous issue will affect the reviewing systems that need to be in place and contained in the *Regulations for Independent Reviewing Officers* (DfES, 2004).

Working relationships between services

As Support Care takes many shapes, and may be based on its own or as part of a children and families team, the fostering service or family support service within a local authority, it is essential to develop protocols and guidance to ensure effective delivery of the service.

Setting up a Support Care service

Part of the work of the Fostering Network Support Care Project will be to draw experiences together and develop information systems specifically targeted at setting up a scheme. This would include information on planning the service, recruitment, assessment, training and support to Support Carers.

Research

It is essential that the development of Support Care is subject to research. An initial research programme was undertaken by the Thomas Coram Research Unit and Institute of Education (Greenfields and Statham, 2004) primarily focusing on the barriers that might be deterring local authorities from establishing Support Care schemes (see Chapter 11). The Fostering Network project plans to continue working with the Thomas Coram Research Unit and Institute for Education to develop further research on Support Care.

Challenging the low status of Support Care

A key part of the project needs to be in raising not only the profile of Support Care but also its importance and value. Evidence collected by The Thomas Coram Research Unit and Institute of Education identified that where Support Care is part of a local authority's strategic plan, ownership and recognition increased; carers were paid more or less in line with mainstream foster carers and capacity existed for development work.

Role of Support Care in relation to family group conferencing

Support Care could increasingly be used as one support option when undertaking family group conferencing as both services put the family at the centre of their thinking. A family group conference is a process where families meet to find solutions to problems they and their children are experiencing, within a professionally supportive framework. The process involves all family members, friends and other adults the family feels can contribute to the plans for their children. Like Support Care, family group conferencing can be used for a variety of situations and is based on the belief that families are in the best position to make informed, culturally-sensitive decisions about their children, provided they are given the opportunity and information to do so.

Post-placement support

There is a range of situations where a child returns home and support is needed. Anecdotal and research evidence (Sinclair, 2004) shows that without good support on returning home families are often not able to sustain reunification and so the cycle of care continues. The Project will explore the viability of Support Care as a post-placement option.

The Fostering Network Support Care Project workers will be supported in their work by a steering group and a specialist consultant, Joy Howard who has extensive experience of developing and managing the Support Care scheme in Bradford (see Chapter 2). The Fostering Network will manage the project. Clearly, the wide brief as set out above requires a national overview and management.

Although primarily used as a response to families in crisis and for children and young people at risk of accommodation, Support Care is also developing in a range of ways as evidenced in the diagram earlier in this chapter. The Fostering Network can provide an overview and promote its varied use.

Conclusion

Support Care is a simple concept that reflects the spirits of the Seebohm Report, the Children Act 1989 and the Children Act 2004. It is flexible and effective but it fits into a complex legal framework. The Fostering Network is in a unique position nationally to promote and influence the development of Support Care. It can bring together the varied applications of Support Care into a flexible model which can be used in a range of situations where families are in crisis and, importantly, to keep Support Care on the Government's agenda and raise its profile at local level through its wide membership base.

The timing is right for a national initiative, to promote Support Care as an essential resource for children and young people and their families, and to assist local authorities to meet their responsibilities as set out in recent government directives.

References

DfES (2001) *Ofsted Regulations*. London: DfES.

DfES (2003b) *Day Care and Child Minding (National Standards) (England) Regulations*. London: The Stationery Office.

DfES (2004) *Independent Reviewing Officers Guidance and Regulations*. London: The Stationery Office.

DoH (1998a) *Modernising Social Services: Promoting Independence, Improving Protection, Raising Standards*. London: The Stationery Office.

DoH (1998) *The Quality Protects Programme: Transforming Children's Services. LAC (98) 28*. London: DoH.

DoH (2000) *Framework for the Assessment of Children in Need and their Families*. London: The Stationery Office.

DoH (2002a) *Fostering Services: National Minimum Standards, Fostering Services Regulations*. London: The Stationery Office.

DoH (2002b) *Choice Protects Programme: Building on Quality Protects Programme, Transforming Children's Services*. London: DoH.

DoH (2002c) *Fostering for the Future: SSI Report of the Inspection of Foster Care Services*. London: DoH.

DoH (2003a) *LAC 13: Guidance on Accommodating Children in Need and their Families*. London: DoH.

DoH (2003b) *HSC 2003/003 – Child and Adolescent Mental Health Service (CAMHS Grant Guidance 2003/04)*. London: DoH.

DoH/DfES (2004) *LASSL 5: Special Grant for the Development of Treatment Foster Care Programmes*. London: DoH/DfES.

DoH, Home Office and DfES (1999) *Working Together to Safeguard Children*. London: HMSO.

HM Treasury (2003a) *Every Child Matters*. London: The Stationery Office.

HM Treasury (2003b) *The Parenting Fund Proposals for Consultation*. London: The Stationery Office.

Laming, H. (2003) *Seebohm Lecture*. Southampton University.

NFCA UK Joint Working Party on Foster Care (1999a) *The UK National Standards for Foster Care*. London: NFCA.

NFCA UK Joint Working Party on Foster Care (1999b) *Code of Practice on the Recruitment, Assessment, Approval, Training, Management and Support for Foster Carers*. London: NFCA.

Seebohm, F. (1968) *Report of the Committee on Local Authority and Allied Personal Social Services*. London: HMSO.

Sinclair, I. (2005) *Fostering Now: Messages from Research*. London: Jessica Kingsley.

United Nations (1989) *United Nations Convention on the Rights of the Child*. New York: UN.

www.doh.gov.uk/integratedchildrenssystem

www.surestart.gov.uk/aboutsurestart

Chapter 2

Partnership With Parents: Making it Happen

Joy Howard

Introduction

Support Care in Bradford is a fully developed family support fostering service, which uses part-time foster carers as short-break providers for families under stress. It is now established as an integral part of a front-line preventative strategy and operates within the Family Support Division of the Social Services Department. This chapter will describe the process of implementation from initial thinking, through to the development of the scheme and its eventual integration into mainstream service provision in Bradford. It will provide a brief outline of how the concept of Support Care has achieved national recognition, and include a profile of use and a discussion of significant practice issues.

Getting started

The Children Act: identifying the need

When this Act finally came into force everywhere there were flurries of activity, training programmes, and new procedures based on fresh thinking. Social work managers and practitioners were excited by the new ideas; the Act was seen as both a challenge and a catalyst for positive change. For me, one of the most radical of the changes in practice that emerged was the concept of partnership with parents. From the perspective of service provision, working in a Fostering Unit, it seemed that we had a real opportunity to re-frame the whole concept of local authority care. The new terms – 'accommodation' and 'looked after' – were created to emphasise the proposed partnership approach.

Efforts were made to reframe accommodation in terms of working alongside parents, but it became clear that in effect this was hard to achieve. To separate young people from their families didn't feel like partnership, and episodes of accommodation were usually still experienced as a family trauma from which it took time and a lot of work to recover. Moreover, at the next time of crisis, families would ask for and expect a similar response. In this way, accommodation becomes the resource of choice. As it was commonly acknowledged that repeated episodes of accommodation led to a drift into long-term care, it was apparent that however the terminology changed, radical new thinking was needed to break the downward spiral.

The problems with accommodation were there; solutions, though, could perhaps be found in looking at the Children Act, and further exploring the concept of partnership. Our Fostering Unit was, for example, frequently being asked to facilitate a gradual return home, based on reducing time spent with a carer until a family felt strong enough to take over again. This entirely reasonable scenario was, and still is an impossible demand for a beleaguered fostering service with not enough placements to go round, and a chronic shortage of new foster carers. As an 'add-on' it was unfeasible; new thinking was needed. In 1992, I wrote a proposal for a specialist scheme, based on the premise that families in crisis needed a more flexible and less dramatic response to the cry for help that can end up becoming a request for accommodation. I felt that families had a right to such services; I was also convinced that many accommodations, and the subsequent potential of drift towards a child or young person becoming looked after by the local authority, could be averted with the introduction of a different kind of intervention at an early stage.

I wanted to set up a scheme in which carers could offer part-time care to children and young people at risk of becoming separated from their families. This would involve a planned series of short breaks, with the aim of reducing tension, creating a breathing space to enable everyone to think through the difficulties and facilitating ongoing family work by introducing a feeling of co-operation and goodwill. Carers would be working alongside families rather than taking over from them. Parents and family carers would retain full responsibility, and children and young people would remain based at home. The aim of the placements would be to support parents in the care of their children, and to ensure that by the time the placement ended, the family home was a more settled and workable environment for parents and children alike. I wrote a discussion paper, backed up by feedback via questionnaires from social work managers and practitioners, with proposals for implementation. This was well received, but unfortunately large-scale internal re-structuring involving all sectors of social services meant that the time was not right to proceed. It was not until four years later that the Department was fully settled and ready to take a fresh look at the idea.

The pilot year

Fostering services management in Bradford gave the go-ahead for a pilot year in April 1996. It was decided that the service would initially be limited to the nine plus age group, as fewer preventative resources were available to older children and young people, especially teenagers. I began work on implementing the scheme; a year later it was up and running, with twelve carers. Over one hundred referrals had been taken, and Support Care was accepted as a valuable resource.

How was it done? Initially, by looking at internal resources in terms of carers already working with the fostering unit, but who were thinking of leaving the service, either because of exhaustion and burn-out after many years of service, or because of feeling inadequate and depressed following a traumatic placement breakdown, or simply because of a change in personal circumstances. Carers were also asked if they would consider an 'add-on' part-time placement to their quota. Temporary changes in terms of approval were negotiated, and a fee structure agreed. Referral and practice procedures were formulated, and the new scheme publicised around the department. In no time at all, it felt like the most popular game in town (Howard, 1997).

From the first, a database was established and everything was carefully recorded. This I saw as an absolute essential if the scheme was to have half a chance of moving beyond the pilot year; the use and effectiveness of the service needed to be demonstrable. The information collected not only proved invaluable in doing just that, but also in allowing for year-on-year comparison, analysis of patterns of use, building up a profile of demand, looking at outcomes. Over subsequent years, it has been an invaluable tool in informing developments and evaluating success.

Moving forward

Building the resource: responding to demand

Over the next three years, Support Care expanded in terms of the recruitment of new carers, the first that were approved specifically to do this work. The concept of flexibility included looking at the amount of time a carer could offer, and using whatever was available to increase the range of options for families in need of a service. As we were all new to the idea at the outset, social workers would typically ask for every other weekend; I suggested this myself on many occasions in the early days. It couldn't last. I was rapidly running out of the ability to respond. I started to ask carers if they would consider some overnights during the week. This suited some people very well. I also asked social workers to try one weekend per month – this too worked well nine times out of ten, and this is now the most usual arrangement; also, interestingly, the one most often requested.

A big breakthrough was initiated when a carer, well known to me, who had worked for Bradford over many years, told me she was leaving because her new partner did not want to be involved in full-time care. It turned out he didn't want to do overnights either. This carer was devastated at the prospect of having to give up the work she loved. I promptly filled up her weekdays and every other Saturday with a selection of boys aged eleven to fifteen that were her favourite group. So successful has she been that though it seemed to be taking a bit of a chance to suggest to social workers that an alternative to their request for a full weekend stay twice a month could be a bit of daycare on Saturdays, this is now also something that is often asked for at the outset. Ever since then, daycare has been an important and well-used part of our service, and has led to the approval of a number of carers doing just that; people who would not previously have been considered for assessment, as day care had not previously been considered as a fostering task in Bradford.

I have learned through experiences like these that an open approach not only leads to expansion in service provision but that less can be more, so costs do not automatically escalate. And also that flexibility, if it includes everyone, can make everyone feel like a winner.

It was important to me that the family-friendly resource I wanted to establish should also be seen as friendly and approachable by family social workers. This was about more than a wish to be seen as 'warm and fluffy' by colleagues 'out there'. I wanted the resource to reflect demand, rather than building a service that people had to be fitted into. It always surprises me that this is seen as a revolutionary concept. It is still almost universally assumed that if you ask people to ask for things, a deluge will follow. Support Care began by doing away with the notion of 'eligibility criteria', and being client-led in its response. There has been no deluge. What has emerged is a lot of goodwill, people being prepared to compromise and do deals, and all-round flexibility. We all give a bit: families, social workers, carers, ourselves. Support Care has gone on as it started, and has grown and developed along the lines defined by the needs of its client group (Howard, 2000; 2005).

Getting established

Placing the service: funding, team building

It took four years to get started. For the next four years, with no dedicated funding available, I ran the scheme virtually single-handed. My experience of setting up and operating within a fostering unit sounds like hard work, and it was. My team colleagues were on the whole supportive, and without their taking on some of the management of individual placements, I could not have developed the service to the extent that I did. But the general feeling was of swimming against the tide. Extremely popular with the family social workers who used the service, but seen as marginal within the fostering unit, Support Care felt wrongly placed. At a subsequent departmental restructure, I was therefore happy with the suggestion that the Service should be re-sited within the newly formed Community Support sector. This felt more like home, closer to the families for whom the service had been developed, and with better links to their social workers. But I was on my own, and rapidly running out of available time to keep all the plates spinning. Although there was no specific budget provision, a part-time resource worker was eventually allocated; it was with this 'team' that Support Care survived through to the arrival of *Quality Protects* (DoH, 1998) and – at last – some dedicated funding.

The remit of the new money was to allow expansion to the nought to eight age group, and provided for the recruitment of a small team, and proper office space, though funding was guaranteed only for a year. This element of uncertainty led to a difficult period. Though we did manage to move things on considerably, it was a constant struggle to maintain a team who, with funding renewals maintained on a temporary basis, could not be expected to have long-term commitment. In 2002, a new Director and Head of Service for Children's Division were appointed. By early 2003, the issues had been taken on board, and decisions on permanent funding were made. However, in the interim all of the original team had left, and the scheme was being held together by a succession of agency workers. The loyalty and commitment of the carers was admirable, and without that Support Care might not have survived.

From the summer of 2003, when the new permanent team was established, things have really come together. More funding has been found to allow us to build extra capacity, including long-term options. The future now looks assured. What emerges so clearly from this history is the importance, in building new projects, of senior management in social services departments having a stake from the earliest opportunity. I am aware of many similar schemes across the country that have fallen by the wayside over the years for the lack of this. Many are now being rebuilt, but much time, energy and money has been wasted.

Potential for development

In spite of all these difficulties however, Support Care has continued to grow. As well as developing a service for the under-eights, spin-off projects have been undertaken. One of these is adoption support, which is described in this book (see Chapter 5). We have also, with the help of dedicated government funding – initially from the Cabinet Office (Social Exclusion Unit), then moving to the Department of Health (Children and Young People's Unit) and finally the Department for Education and Skills – set up a scheme that allows us to respond more effectively to urgent need. Crisis Care was developed specifically to ensure provision for young runaways, but it can also provide an overnight stay in a situation where a young person can not return home that night. It has proved to be so useful that Bradford has decided to take it over as a mainstream resource. Meanwhile, additional government funding has been secured, to allow for expansion over a further two-year period, and incorporate the building of closer links with other agencies working with both missing young people and families in conflict.

We have begun to address the issue of longer-term need. For some families, the difficulties are chronic, and it is difficult to set an agenda for change that is meaningful within a limited time framework. Most commonly, this is around health issues, either for a child/young person or for a parent/family carer. But there are also instances where a family has such a history of poor parenting that care proceedings would be considered if support were to be withdrawn. Support Care can help if we are prepared to add long-term options to our repertoire. It is my view that were general fostering resources to develop the concept of shared care – foster carers sharing the care of children and young people with their families – social workers need not be faced with the choice of either living with too much risk or finding a permanent foster or residential home for their young people. An alternative could be offered that would avoid all the traumas of family breakdown, and introduce stability, monitoring and parenting support to families in severe difficulties. Most young people return home on leaving care, but to a fractured family. Sharing the care would allow for the possibility of change for the better within the family, and deliver improved long-term outcomes for young people. Support Care has shown the way. We have begun work on looking at the situations of young people already in long-term care, to see whether a return home would be viable if such an arrangement were in place. We have also demonstrated that there is a new pool of potential foster carers out there who will take on work with the whole family, and who have not presented themselves in the past because they are not able to commit to full-time fostering.

Two smaller-scale developments are worth mentioning. Firstly, our summer holiday, caravan, scheme is highly valued. We have been able to offer a seaside holiday, with our carers, to nearly fifty young people over the past four years. A second spin-off has been the retention of two carers, no longer able to offer time and space in their own homes, but attracted by a new career as sessional workers with young people. This has proved to be a very useful add-on, and a great way of retaining the services of skilled carers who would otherwise have had to resign.

Adoptive parents are a specialist group, with particular needs. Over the last two years, a longer-term pilot scheme was set up within Support Care. This has now been transferred to the new Adoption Support team in Bradford (see Chapter 5).

Playing away

Publicity

So successful and so rewarding was Support Care turning out to be that after the first two years I wanted to share the news and hopefully persuade colleagues in other local authorities to join in. I wrote an article for a widely read, social care, magazine (Howard, 1999) and the response was amazing. The phone kept on ringing: there were people who had just started something similar, and had thought themselves alone; people who were excited by the idea and wanted to know all about how to do it; and people who had been doing something similar for a while, were still committed but feeling unsupported and at risk of being closed down. From this, and from following up other leads, I rapidly built up an extensive contact list. It was time to get all these people together.

Partnership

From the very early days, the Fostering Network (then the National Foster Care Association) responded with enthusiasm, and has remained keen to promote the ideas of Support Care. The scheme featured in their series of 'good practice' manuals. By 2000, I was also in contact with the University of Bradford in connection with a small piece of evaluative research that I had requested. A partnership was formed for the purpose of planning a national conference. So, almost exactly five years from embarking on the pilot year, 60 delegates arrived in Bradford to take part in a day of discussion, practice sharing and making links (NFCA, 2001). This event marked the beginning of a new phase. It felt as though Support Care had become a movement and that as a movement it had achieved critical mass, and was unstoppable.

Following the 2001 conference, Lloyd's TSB funding was obtained by the Fostering Network for a two-year project to publicise the work, disseminate information and lobby for government backing. We spoke at conferences, ran a series of regional seminars, increased our network of contacts by one hundred per cent, and significantly raised the profile of Support Care within government. Recommendations about implementing Support Care schemes were made as part of the 2003 Choice Protects Review and at the same time the DoH commissioned research to examine barriers to implementation in local authorities around the UK (Greenfields and Statham, 2004) (see Chapter 11).

Further funding, this time from the Department of Education and Skills will ensure that the momentum gained will continue. This is certain to be reinforced by implementation of the Children Act 2004 emphasising, as it does, the need for preventative work with families (see Chapter 1).

Looking back

Who has been helped?

Over the years, the profile of use, in Bradford, has remained remarkably consistent, with the largest user group in terms of parents and family carers being single mothers, with grandparents also forming an increasingly significant proportion of the whole. The figures for children and young people show a preponderance of young men in the nine to thirteen age bracket. This group comprises sixty to seventy per cent of referrals. There has been an increase in the number of young women referred, and the most prominent age group here is thirteen to fifteen. Clusters of significant factors in referrals indicate that adolescent conflict with parents has a huge impact, often compounded by problems at school, and mental health difficulties, either for the parent or young person. As we have only been offering a service to the nought to eight age group for the last two years, the overall picture is still emerging; year-on-year analysis will give clearer indicators (Howard, 2000; 2005).

It has been a concern from the start that the numbers of referrals from Black and Ethnic Minority groups has been disproportionally low. This is not a phenomenon exclusive to Bradford (Richards and Wilson, 2000) but given that South Asian communities alone comprise around thirty per cent of the city's population, this was a local issue that needed to be urgently addressed. In 2002, a grant from the Children's Fund allowed us to commission a small research project with a brief to explore some of the reasons for the lack of take up among families from South Asian Communities. The findings were informative and gave us the impetus and sense of direction that was needed. We recruited a number of carer families, and are now in a position to publicise our work and invite referrals. Links with Sure Start look to be a positive way forward.

Meanwhile it is worth noting that we are making a small but significant difference in the area of identity issues for young people of dual or multiple heritages. Our Black and South Asian carers offer an ongoing befriending service which allows young people to maintain or rediscover a sense of cultural belonging, at their own pace and in a very unforced way. We have seen that a little can go a very long way indeed in these instances, and that white parents of dual heritage children can also gain a lot from the connections made.

Figures 2.1 to 2.7 below give an overview of the categories of referrals in relation to: request; age and gender of the child or young person; ethnicity; significant factors in referrals and the makeup of families in need of Support Care between 2001 and 2004.

How have we done it? The following basic principles underlie all our practice.

Approachability

Demand-led from the start, as already described, the imposition of eligibility criteria has been resisted. Two-way communication and mutual respect have been key. To this end, no applications for a resource are taken on paper. Every referral starts with a conversation; this avoids unnecessary follow-up, and ensures clarity of purpose from the outset. Some conversations end in agreement that Support Care may not be the way forward, some result in

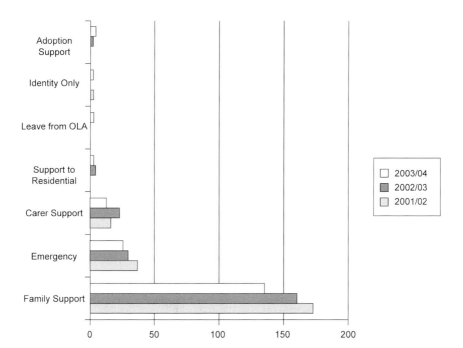

Figure 2.1   Category of request

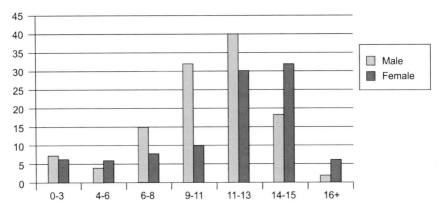

Figure 2.2 Age/gender 2001/2002

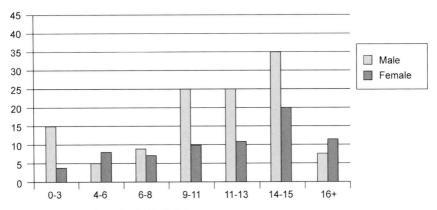

Figure 2.3 Age/gender 2002/2003

different thinking from the initial request, compromise solutions are discussed. A piece of paper requesting a resource, a 'referral' form, implies a fixed request, and an expectation that it will be filled-disappointment often follows. It is hard to build up goodwill that way, and stand-off scenarios can develop. A referral taken from a conversation allows for flexibility and understanding all round. Our evaluations demonstrate that this approach is appreciated – we are seen as open and helpful; even if we can't always produce the goods, we are known as people who will try hard to do so. Another spin-off is that social workers and the families they serve are prepared to wait for a resource. Because we never say no (unless by mutual agreement), and almost always come back with a placement offer eventually, we have become an organisation that is trusted and respected throughout the department, as we have learnt from both verbal and written feedback.

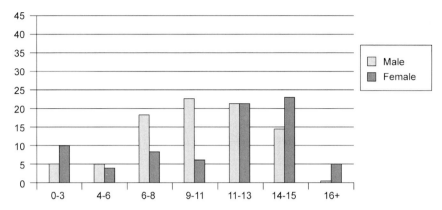

Figure 2.4 Age/gender 2003/2004

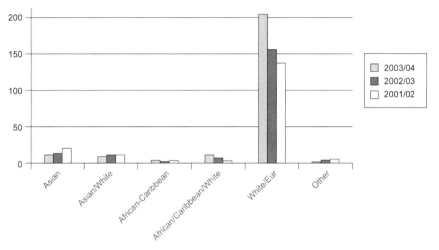

Figure 2.5 Ethnicity

Respect for service users

Most families have ups and downs; most families have resources to call on to help them through. For those that need help from social services, delivery of that help should be as non-blaming, non-stigmatising, respectful and enabling as possible (DoH, 1991; Ghate and Hazel, 2003; Quinton, 2004). Parents and family carers, and children and young people, are for this reason fully involved in all the decision-making throughout the process. The resource is not an imposed, but a chosen solution. There is a shared assumption from the start that Support Care will not be needed for longer

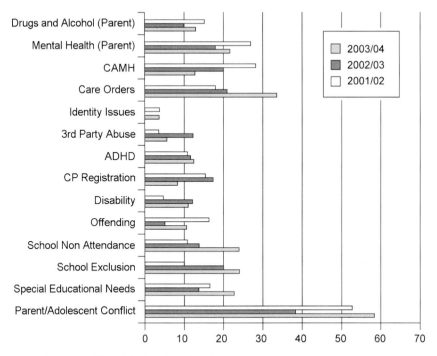

Figure 2.6 Significant factors in referral

than a few months. This reinforces the message that people are not viewed as 'bad parents': simply that it is understood that parenting is a difficult task for all parents, and that these particular ones are going through a rough patch. This is also an essential message to give to the children and young people involved, many of whom have low self-esteem, lack confidence and are fearful of 'going into care'. Interestingly, from their comments, it seems that neither parents nor young people view stays with support carers as 'care', even though, technically, the arrangements do fall under Section 20, and are therefore, strictly speaking, local authority accommodations.

Support Care in action really does feel like partnership. It is good to engage in joint problem-solving with colleagues who are family work caseholders. Joint decision-making, together with families and carers is also crucial, but neither tells the whole story. What makes the placements special are the relationships established between carers and parents. Typically these are friendly, unthreatening and respectful. This creates scope for carers to offer advice to parents that is seen as helpful rather than interfering, and therefore

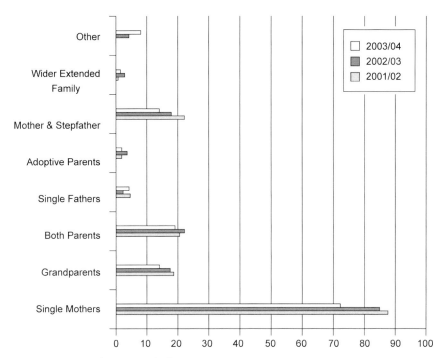

Figure 2.7 Families in need of resource

likely to be acted upon, and even sought. For children and young people it is greatly beneficial to find themselves in a situation where the adults in their lives are working together to sort things out. It is the carers and parents who really deliver the benefits of partnership on the ground.

It is significant that parents, however demanding or needy they are described to be at the time of referral, rarely take advantage of the situation by not keeping to agreements, or asking for more. This has to be about being treated with respect, staying in control, and feeling helped. Goodwill and trust have been established, and this is not thrown away lightly by anyone. Endings are mutually agreed. Some families are re-referred a year or so down the line – this is to be expected given the premise that family life is not a smooth progress, and more help may be needed from time to time. Repeat referrals often involve a different, more low-key and shorter timescale response. It is a compliment to Support Care that parents have found from us the help they needed – we should not turn down a request for more when it is needed again.

The Children Act revisited

Two or three years ago, while looking for a useful quote from the legislation, I had a trawl through the Children Act Guidance and Regulations with respect to partnership with parents. Though the Act had been a trigger for initiating the Service, I had not often referred back to the detail over the years. I was surprised and delighted to find that Support Care was following the letter as well as the spirit of the Act in almost every respect. As family support policies have developed exponentially since 1997, it was a strong reminder of the fundamental philosophical change that the concept of partnership with parents had heralded in the previous decade.

The Act's philosophy is that the best place for children to be brought up is within their own family, and that children in need can be helped most effectively if the local authority, working in partnership with parents, provides an appropriate range and level of services.

Key recommendations included the following:

- On accommodation: *arrangements [should] assist and enhance, not undermine, the parent's authority and control* (DoH, 1991: 5).
- On assessment: *Families . . . have the right to receive sympathetic support and sensitive intervention* (DoH, 1991: 6).
- On service provision: *The emphasis will . . . build upon the families strengths and minimise any weaknesses* (DoH, 1991: 11).
- On consultation: *Partnership requires informed participation . . . during the decision-making process* (DoH, 1991: 11).
- On review objectives: *Every effort should be made to enhance the parents capabilities and confidence* (DoH, 1991: 11).

There are many more – but to conclude, a quote that seems to summarise quite beautifully the ideological underpinning of Support Care:

> *In general, families have the capacity to cope with their own problems, or identify and draw on resources in the community for support. Some families reach a stage where they are not able to resolve their difficulties . . . and may look to social services for support and assistance . . . they should receive a positive response which reduces any fears . . . of stigma or loss of parental responsibility.*
>
> (DoH, 1991: 8)

There you have it.

Looking forward

Expansion: Bradford and beyond

Support Care in Bradford is now a highly valued resource with an assured future; it seems likely that it will expand and become even stronger. New developments will doubtless come along in response to need, as has been the case to date. One hoped-for development should be the forging of stronger links locally with health and education; there is insufficient joined-up working and thinking at present, and it could only be of benefit to the people we serve if we could work together more coherently. The development of Children's Trusts should certainly speed up this process. Joint working could do much to push forward the agenda of de-stigmatisation. Referrals from universal services such as GP surgeries and schools would have a different feel, and one that might particularly encourage families from minority ethnic communities to ask for help. We have learned from the research we have commissioned, as well as from partners such as Sure Start, that such institutions are highly regarded, particularly within South Asian communities in Bradford. By contrast, it seems that trust in social services provision is low, and engagement with them seen as stigmatising.

On a national level, a properly organised network will be a key task for the future. There are now over two hundred contacts nation-wide, and the first newsletter was distributed last year. The ideas of Support Care have begun to inform thinking in social services departments around the country, but new projects are always vulnerable species, and strength in numbers will be crucial to their success. It will also be an important task to try and ensure a cohesive approach, in the sense of shared good practice; included will be discussions with the Department of Education and Skills on the thorny issue of legal status. Sections 20 and 17, currently the norm, are neither of them particularly suited to Support Care or other short break schemes. New regulations, if achievable, would be the preferred outcome.

There are now twenty or more Support Care schemes across the UK. Some have been around for a while, and descriptions of their work will be found elsewhere in this book (see Chapters 6, 8, 9 and 10). The close co-operation and expanding involvement of the Fostering Network, together with encouragement from government following on new research findings (see Chapter 11) are good indicators that the rolling out of new schemes will increase year on year. Again, the Children Act 2004, with its re-focusing on prevention and renewal of emphasis on family support will be a crucial factor.

It is immensely rewarding to review the last twelve years, and see the progress of an idea from personal brainchild to national agenda. It has also been a continual source of encouragement to discover that others have had similar ideas, and in some cases, similar struggles to get them across. We will all now benefit from being on the map and part of a cohesive movement for change.

References

DoH (1991) *The Children Act 1989 Guidance and Regulations, Volume 2, Family Support, Day Care and Educational Provision for Young children.* London: HMSO.

DoH (1998) *The Quality Protects Programme: Transforming Children's Services. LAC (98) 28.* London: DoH.

Ghate, D. and Hazel, N. (2002) *Parenting in Poor Environments: Stress, Support and Coping.* London: Jessica Kingsley.

Greenfields, M. and Statham, J. (2004) *Support Foster Care: Developing a Short-Break Service for Children in Need. Understanding Children's Social Care Series. 8.* London: Institute of Education, University of London.

Howard, J. (1997) *A Caring Alternative: Building a New Resource for Young People in Need and their Families.* Bradford: Bradford MDC, Department of Social Services.

Howard, J. (1999) Take a Break. *Community Care.* 1271: 18.

Howard, J. (2000) Support Care: A New Role for Foster Carers. In Wheal, A. (Ed.) *Working with Parents: Learning from Other People's Experience.* Lyme Regis: Russell House Publishing.

Howard, J. (2005) Support Care. In Wheal, A. (Ed.) *The RHP Companion to Foster Care.* Lyme Regis: Russell House Publishing.

National Foster Care Association (2001) *Support Care: Foster Carers and Parents in Partnership.* Report of the Conference held in April at the University of Bradford. London: NFCA.

Quinton, D. (2004) *Supporting Parents: Messages from Research.* London: Jessica Kingsley.

Richards, A. and Wilson, L. (2000) *Overcoming the Obstacles: Looked After Children: Quality Services for Black and Minority Ethnic Children and their Families.* London: Family Rights Group.

Further reading

Aldgate, J. and Bradley, M. (1999) *Supporting Families through Short-term Fostering.* London: HMSO.

Laws, S. and Broad, B. (2000) *Looking after Children Within the Extended Family: Carer's Views.* Leicester: De Montfort University, Department of Social and Community Studies.

Richards, A. (2001) *Second Time Around: A Survey of Grandparents Raising their Grandchildren.* London: Family Rights Group.

ATD Fourth World (1996) *Talk With Us Not At Us: How to Develop Partnerships between Families in Poverty and Professionals.* London: ATD Fourth World.

Chapter 3

Staying in Control

Joanne Bell

Introduction

In this chapter I, as a parent who has accessed Support Care in Bradford, describe my experiences as a parent seeking help.

When you are given your baby and it's put into your arms, you think everything is magical and life is a bed of roses. What you don't realise is you are beginning on the hardest part of your life, the happiest and the saddest. I noticed that things were not going as I had hoped, when I was working full-time, as was my husband. My son was starting to get into trouble. Initially it was telling lies – only little ones at first. Then he was having fights at school with other children for apparently no reason at all. By the time my son was seven years old I had to take him out of his primary school because of his behaviour. He was ignoring the school rules and getting into trouble.

At his next school I thought things would be better. I went to my GP to ask for help. I was told not to worry, as he would grow out of it. In less than three months, my son had managed to get himself excluded from school. The fighting had got a lot worse and his behaviour had become unacceptable. He had even run away from the school when he knew he was in trouble. Back to the doctor's I went, but, instead of coming away with nothing, I stood there and argued my case: that my son needed help for his anger, help to learn that if things went wrong it could be because of his behaviour or attitude to people.

A referral for help

While my son was not at school his problems were much less – perhaps from a quarter to half of what was happening when he was in school. His anger seemed to quieten down and his attitude improved a lot. I then was sent a letter to take my son to a Child and Adolescent Unit, to see a psychotherapist for counselling. I thought to myself that all my problems were over, because a professional person would be able to see what I was talking about. We were going to the Unit once a month. My son attended another school, but once again the problems reoccurred. He would get into fights for no reason at all, he would argue with the teachers all the time. His lies were really bad; and also he was stealing anything he could lay his hands on. I was told he was a very bright young man and maybe he was just bored. This did not go down very well, as the school was calling me in at least once a week due to my son's behaviour, which was now trying everyone's patience.

At one point when we were at the Unit I did not know who was the patient and who was the psychologist, as my son could play mind games with the professional better than the other way round. I remember the psychologist once actually said, 'When he is misbehaving, get a broom and tell him to put his head on the top and run round it in circles for five minutes.' When I enquired why? he replied, 'Well, it might work, and if it doesn't it will keep him quiet for 10 minutes.' When I asked him what was wrong with my son, he told me he had a 'conduct disorder'. It felt like a professional's label, a coverall, and it didn't tell me anything new. After one and a half years, I asked to see someone else, as I felt that we were getting nowhere. Two months after talking to the Manager and proving that my son was playing games, I got a new psychologist.

Someone new

My son would choose different themes for his behaviour over the months. One week he would tell lies until he could go no further. Then he would steal things until he couldn't get away with that any more. I could predict, to a certain degree, when things were really sliding, what avenue he would choose. Things were getting worse though; I felt I could not cope with any more of my son's behaviour at school, or at home. I was trying to keep a full-time job, and cope with whatever my son decided to try, as each week could be different. In one month he stole the teacher's car keys, stole money from a family member, and was suspended four times from school. He threatened to cut his wrists with some glass, and his attitude was deteriorating towards everyone.

I had been thinking of ringing Bradford Social Services, but thought that they would only take my son away and I didn't want the shame of everyone knowing that I was dealing with social services. I thought you had to be the worst person or mother going, to get involved with them. You had to harm your child or children or to be totally unfit. These were my views at the time, as I had never had anything to do with social services before. I only knew what I had read in the papers or had seen on the television.

At this point I did not know where to turn. I had heard the odd whisper in the playground when I was collecting my son, as people can be so cruel and judgmental about what they do not understand. I had tried to speak to my friends about my son's behaviour, but they just said they did not want my son playing with their children, and then talked behind my back. I felt so low. I was a failure at being a mum, and my son's behaviour was my problem, as I must have somehow caused it. I could feel myself sinking into depression. I would cry over anything and then get angry at the slightest thing. I was still working in spite of all the pressures on me. I was called out of work to go and pick my son up from school at least once a week. So I decided to start nightshifts to keep my job. I would take my son to school, then go home to bed. If I did not get a 'phone call from school, I would sleep till two-thirty in the afternoon then get up to collect my son. I would walk down to the school door to be met by a teacher saying, 'Could we just have a word with you?' How I hated those words. I used to hang my head and feel so ashamed, as if *I* had committed an offence. I would see people whispering, and laughing saying, 'We know who that's about.' At this point I felt paranoid: I believed that the school, doctors, friends, family were judging me on everything I did. This was the worst feeling I have ever had. Every time I made a decision, I questioned myself time and time again hoping that I would get it right. I was full of self-doubt, and feeling out of control and heading for disaster.

A mum's dilemma

I now reached the point I hope no mum has to reach. I knew if I did not get help I would end up in a mental hospital, or I would harm my son who I still loved very much. I just could not reach him to tell him how much he was hurting me and everyone around him. At the Child and Adolescent Unit they said they were 'making progress'. The only thing was neither the school nor I could see it. One day I had finally had enough and rang Bradford Social Services. To my surprise, they would not come out and see me straight away. I was told I had to wait for an appointment, which could take as much as a couple of months. I felt I could not go on any more so I told them if they did not come out I would kill my child. I thought that would give me priority, and then they would come and take my son away, and I could just rest for a few days, and sleep. At this time I was so low and depressed that I didn't really think anyone could help either my son or me. I was losing control.

I went back to my GP but he could not do anything as my son was still officially being treated by the Child and Adolescent Unit, though they weren't seeing him very often any more. The doctor said he could not 'intervene', but gave me some sleeping tablets. As my son had attempted to set his bedroom on fire, the last thing I felt I should be taking were sleeping tablets.

Today is the day of all days I remember thinking, because social services were coming to my house. I was dreading the meeting, the shame that all of the street would know I was a failed mother. I remember looking up and down the street for these aliens with banners saying *Here's another unfit mother* (by this time I think I was paranoid). I watched as a car pulled up outside my house, and a normal man and woman got out. My heart racing, I ran to the door, opened it and nearly dragged them in, because I could not do with the shame.

They were very nice and apologised to me for having to wait to see them, but they had been inundated with calls. We spoke for about an hour, and they said they would get me a family resource worker.

Help at last

Within the month a lady called Maggie got in touch. She started to work with my son, and after a couple of months she asked if she could pick my son up from school and also go into the school to talk with the teachers. I agreed because the phone calls were getting more frequent and my son was being sent home more regularly. Maggie set up some meetings with the people concerned. I still did not tell anyone that social services were involved. I was still carrying the guilt and shame with me so I could not walk with my head up high. Maggie did take a lot of pressure off me by being involved with the school and coming in for meetings.

Maggie started to collect my son from school and take him back to her offices to work with him. One day my son was missing when Maggie went to the school. We both searched for him for over two hours, and then I went home and reported him missing to the police. He turned up at his Nan's house; she was the person who looked after him when he was not at school. He said he had been abducted from just outside school, that cellophane had been put over his mouth and he had woken up behind a building and then made his way back. The police came straight out to the house. They went to search the area and found out he had been at a friend's house playing all the time. Confronted with this he was still insisting that he was telling the truth. After four hours he told us that it was all lies (which we had, of course, already worked out).

Back at the Child and Adolescent Unit I was told that there was nothing basically wrong with my son, but that they would test him for ADHD (Attention Deficit Hyperactivity Disorder). They tested him and concluded that he did not have it as 'he could concentrate now and again if he wanted to'. At this time I felt like I was banging my head against a wall. Except for Maggie, I had no one to turn to. She was still trying to help, and suggested that I could do with some breaks. She explained the Support Care scheme to me and then went off to do the paperwork.

Support care

It was up to me whether I took it or not. Maggie came back to me a week later and said that she had had an offer, and if I wanted to take it up I could meet the people, with my son, in a week's time. I explained that I would like to meet the people first, without my son, to explain to them what was happening. This was agreed, and I went to talk to the carers who would look after my son. I found them to be ordinary people who had a son of their own, and that my house rules were the same as theirs. My son would only get treats when his behaviour had been the best it could be. They agreed they would inform me if they were thinking about giving him a treat. They suggested coming to the house so that they could talk to me while my son got ready. When he was ready they would take him to their house; he would have tea there and stop overnight, as they would be taking him to school the next morning. But this was only if we all agreed. All the time this was happening, nobody was trying to tell me how, what or when I should be doing things. It was my decision. I was still in control.

The meeting was set up, and everything was explained to us all. Then we all signed a contract, which would be reviewed in three months time, or before if needed. My son began visiting every Wednesday. This was the best thing that had come out of the bad experiences with my son. When Wednesday came, the tension and stress would start to come down to a normal level for all of us. Instead of things carrying on and snowballing, we knew that Wednesday was a break, and we could get a rest from each other and calm down. This is one of the most important things that anyone needs in this position. To be able to calm down and have a chance to look at how things are going and from a different side. To be able to think about the best way to deal with a problem. To be able to have time to yourself, and relax (my way was to get into a hot bubble bath with a glass of wine and a good book). Just to have that little bit of space and not worry about the next twelve hours meant such a lot. It also meant I got a really good night's sleep.

The next day, we would all look forward to seeing each other, as we'd had the time to calm down. We realised that we had missed each other but most of all how much we loved each other. Things started to become a lot easier and more settled. My son was still getting into trouble but not as much, and because of the break it didn't feel that it was constant. We all managed to get a rest once a week, which meant that we could build up the strength to go on. The shame of social services being involved lifted a lot because when my son went to the carer it felt like he was going to a relative or a good friend's house. Things were going great for some months. Then my son went off the rails again at school and ended up running away for three days. When we got him back he didn't want to go back to school. We decided to keep him at home for a few months, and teach him his lessons ourselves. The school backed us up, and prepared the work for us. This meant I had to give up my job, which put more pressure on the family.

On a Monday I would go into school to get the work, and would teach my son all week so he didn't fall behind. This became very stressful, and everyone was feeling the strain. Maggie spoke to Joy, who was in charge of Support Care. She suggested my son should go to another carer, during the day, instead of overnight. For the first month, he carried on going to the first carers while he got used to the new arrangement. This was fantastic, as it showed how flexible everyone could be, which at this time I really needed. I felt that, out of all the services involved, this was the only one listening and changing the terms to fit us. My son went during the day to another carer who was just as good as the first carers. At the end of the day they only had the same concerns as I did, and that was to keep my son from going into care, and to help build up the family unit again. They still emphasised that I had the control and they would never try to take that from me.

After three months of my son going to his support carer during the day, and between us gradually returning my son to school, we all felt that it was time for the placement to come to an end. This was sad, as we had got to know each other well. But Support Care had done what it had set out to do, and that was to keep my son at home, to help us rebuild our family life, to develop our confidence in ourselves and to teach us different techniques in how we see each other. We were informed that if we ever got into a family crisis again, then just to ask the social worker to put us back on the list. Knowing this you don't feel like the support has gone and it gives you more confidence to move forward and get on with your life.

Looking forward

Without this service, I am sure my son would have been in care, and the family unit would most certainly have broken down for good. I feel indebted, because they listened, helped, understood, never told us what to do but showed us a way forward when we were all giving up hope. Support Care was our life raft and will be I know to a lot of other people. I have written this in the hope that people will understand and see how desperate family life can be. I could never thank enough the people who helped me keep my family together. They helped us through one of the worst times in our lives.

I want to end by saying as strongly as I can how much I value this service and what an impact I can see it having on the lives of many families struggling to stay together. I would like to see every social services department, up and down the country, having flexible and freely available family-friendly schemes, like the one in Bradford.

Chapter 4

Giving Parents a Lifeline

Janet Exley

Introduction

In this chapter, as a Bradford support carer of many years standing I describe my experience of supporting families and caring for young people, and identify some of the rewards (and occasional difficulties) of the job.

How it started

I became a support carer in Bradford following four years of being a full-time foster carer. I am a single parent with a son aged seventeen, who has been helpfully and happily involved with me in fostering since he was six years old.

At the time of the launch of Support Care I was seriously considering giving up fostering. I'd had a particularly challenging boy for eighteen months, who'd had many disappointments and was becoming exceedingly demanding, so much so that my own son was saying he wanted to go and live with his father if this boy was to stay any longer. I remember myself at the time having immense difficulty trying to find another carer who might be able to help me out and take this boy off my hands from time to time. I needed a break; my son needed a break, so we could spend a little positive time together. My link worker told me about the new scheme, and put me forward for a place. I was offered a weekend every month, and it seemed like a lifesaver. Unfortunately the difficulties and disappointments for my foster child didn't go away, in fact things for him reached a real crisis point not long after. Social Services recognised that he needed specialist residential care, and he was moved away from Bradford.

Feeling worn out and wanting a serious break from being a foster carer I really was considering leaving the service permanently. Joy Howard, the Co-ordinator of the Bradford Support Care Scheme heard about this, and came to see me. She explained how Support Care worked, mostly with families in crisis so as to prevent children coming into care in the first place, and she asked me to think about trying this rather than leaving fostering altogether. It was the perfect solution for me. I really did want to carry on as a foster carer but not on a full-time basis. This way I could dedicate as much or as little time as was best for me. Times to suit me, days to suit me, girls, boys, whatever fitted happily and comfortably into my family's lifestyle. I could have that time with my son, family and friends and was in control of what I took on. I remember thinking – what a fantastic idea! I'd been in a position where I'd desperately needed just that, someone to just now and again help out. This service would be so appreciated, so valuable to families in crisis. I was convinced. I spoke to my son about it and he thought it was a much better idea – that way we got to have lots of children coming and going, and if it turned out he didn't get on with anyone, well at least it would only be for a short time. This could be seen as negative perhaps, but I thought it was realistic and sensible.

So I joined Support Care, and seven years down the line I take great pride in being part of a brilliant team of people who really do help keep families together. It's great to be turning that old-fashioned stigma about social services on its head, the one that says *they take your children away*. We keep families together, whenever and wherever possible.

The formalities

I think a lot to do with the success of Support Care is the way in which it is set up and introduced to families. Parents are always made to feel in control of any decisions concerning their child. The children themselves are involved as much as possible, right up to signing the relevant documents to say they agree with what has been arranged. It's all so positive – by the time the young person comes to stay, they've already met you, and they are OK with it. Parents are feeling comfortable too. The only pressure anyone is feeling is the pressure that is being lifted off. Families are finally getting some practical help.

As a Support Carer, I initially receive details of a child through the post. I am approached about children whom the Support Care team feel are best suited to me. From there I meet the social worker of the young person, so as to talk in more detail about the situation. I feel it best to ask for as much information as I can; it does help. It's OK to say no, and sometimes I do if I feel the child will not fit in and enjoy our lifestyle, or if the difficulties are those I don't feel so well qualified to handle. Having said that, social services have taken all this into account prior to offering you a placement, so usually their suggestions of who comes to you are a good match. Having learnt enough to make a decision, if it is to go ahead a meeting is arranged with the young person and the relevant adults in their lives at the time. This could be mum, dad, grandma, whoever is caring for the child.

These visits are informal, and friendly, and they do break down barriers. They give everybody concerned the opportunity to get a feel for things. A short time is given to enable the family to go away and think about it, and if they agree it would be a suitable placement, we meet up again to discuss the aims of the placement and arrange the actual dates of stays. These can vary from, maybe, after school care, day care, overnights, weekends, whatever is required. Support Care is a tailor-made service, it's flexible, and can be designed to suit every individual family's needs.

Sometimes it is hard to ask for help, and it is hard for parents to bring their children to a stranger's house, and leave them in their care. The introductions plan Support Care follows does eliminate a lot of these worries. Parents see we are not judging them; we are there to support them. The children tend to relax much more because they start to see me as just a mum and a friend rather than a Social Worker or someone in authority. So the visits are planned and set up to go ahead by which time the young person is usually not reluctant at all about coming, in fact have been looking forward to it.

There are many reasons for families needing Support Care. It's not necessarily always because of children's behavioural problems, though that's there most of the time. Sometimes it's about problematic lifestyles; some-times it's just that there is a lack of support in the immediate family. It could be children with ADHD (Attention Deficit Hyperactivity Disorder) or learning difficulties, problems at school, or getting into trouble with the law – there are numerous reasons for families getting stressed out. Each placement is different, and some are more demanding than others are. Each case is reviewed regularly, so that family members and carers get together to discuss how things are going; this way the problems feel shared.

There are tough times too. For as much as we are there to help families, the Social Services Support Care Team are there to help us. I've devoted around twelve years of my life to supporting families and children one way or another, and I've made mistakes. No one is perfect, as carers we can sometimes get things wrong, and it doesn't make us bad people – just maybe a bit naïve or inexperienced. Like all foster carers we have to be aware, for example, that there is a chance of allegations being made against us. It doesn't matter if there is absolutely no truth in them; it can still be crushing. It takes your job away from you while investigations (quite rightly) take place. In this position, you actually welcome an investigation – anything to sort it out – but emotionally the in-between time is tough. The Support Care team is so very sympathetic about this sort of thing. They are so understanding of how we, as carers, must feel and are so supportive. They work hard to get to the bottom of things quickly, so you won't feel dreadful for any longer than necessary.

You can't prepare yourself for things like this really, and it can get you down. It's at times like this you need the support yourself, and the team are there to talk to, to encourage you to be patient, to build you back up again. It's not just the big things. They are there for us whatever the problem, however large or small. They are only a telephone call away, and never make you feel something is too trivial to ask advice on.

Families in crisis

I'm often asked how I get on with parents, and do they feel I'm doing a better job than they are? Do they feel like failures? Do they get jealous if their children go home singing my praises? Of course I want the young people to be happy, of course I want them to feel comfortable and safe during their visits. I talk quite openly from the initial meetings to parents, mums usually, I tell them I'm just a mum like them at the end of the day, I'm not involved in or going through what they are, so who am I to judge. All I want to do is support them in their time of need; offer help and advice where I can and re-assure them that any decisions made are agreed and controlled by them. I'm very careful not to put myself forward as being a better parent than they are. I try to emphasise how all parents have difficulties; it's not unique to them.

As support carers we are asked for advice in many ways by parents. It's funny how all of a sudden we are perceived to be mines of information where children are concerned. Of course we work closely with families and it is nice to know parents (or grandparents) are comfortable enough to discuss their concerns with us. We might not have all the answers but we may have different suggestions, ones we might offer our friends if they were to ask us. Sometimes just talking and not particularly even solving everything can be a huge help; after all we both share and care about the same person at the end of the day.

I'm sure many parents must feel so guilty initially about placing their children in any sort of care. I'm sure they will feel in a sense like they have failed as parents because it has come to this. They will worry about whether their son or daughter is OK with me despite being quite desperate for a break from them. I have a lot of admiration and sympathy for parents, and do my best to reassure them that Social Services are there to help, we are there to help. I really do make an effort to let them know that in no way do I judge them; they have done the best thing asking for help. I'm just a mum too at the end of the day, same as them.

It's not easy to get help when you're having problems in your family and friends often don't want to put up with the hassle it brings. Then if you have no extended family to help out, it can be very isolating. One thing I've found as a support carer is that we do get the best of the children in our care. Their problems don't involve us, we have taken them out of that situation, and they are escaping their troubles for a while. Generally speaking, you seldom see the same sort of behaviour you know is displayed at home.

Being a support carer makes you aware how much of a lifeline you can be to families, but it's very important for parents to know they are still in control of decisions that affect them and the future of their children. It's the basis of a good relationship. I have had few problems with any of the family members of children I've looked after: in fact I am still in contact with some of them, and we've become friends. Some people prefer to draw a line under things when a placement has come to an end – that's OK too. It's a very natural process.

My own family

Your own children do play a part too in being a friend, sharing their things, and sharing you. My son has been fantastic. Of course there have been difficult times – he has had things stolen and damaged, so have I and it's not nice, but that's the nature of the job at times. I've always said to my son that if he didn't want me to do this job I won't, because it's his home too. But he has met lots of young people his age that we've had to stay and he's enjoyed it; some have gone on to be good friends long after the placement is ended.

You have to consider as well that your own children will hear about and see things that they won't even have considered before in their lives. Sometimes these things can be amusing, but some can be a shock. A lot of youngsters are guarded about their feelings and experiences, and of course, part of the job is encouraging them to open up, but when you get the odd one who is really outspoken from the first, it can be hard to take and distressing. You have to prepare your own children, as best you can, and help them understand. It's especially important to do this because the other side of the coin is that young people will often confide in another young person rather than an adult. This is a positive, and my son has experienced this quite often. In fact, a lot of the time your children are your eyes and ears. It is important though that you do prepare your family, particularly the children, to keep you aware of information youngsters may confide in them. It's a tricky one to get right for everybody.

I remember when my son nearly launched a rescue bid for one girl who was unhappy where she was after she'd moved from us. His concern was making him genuinely upset. He's also made really good friends with some of the boys I've looked after – he's even gone to stay at their houses at weekends once they have returned home. Recently I came home to find my son having a laugh and a catch up with a teenager I'd looked after over two years ago. This lad does come periodically and it's lovely to see him, although he is a one-person tornado. He's broken our basketball net, trapped the wire in my toaster and blown it up, and he breaks plates like he's in some Greek Taverna. You just can't get mad with him though; he's got one of those faces.

It warms me to see how he's grown, how many things have changed, how well he's doing. One of the things I noticed more than anything though was how considerate he was toward me and how he treated me with respect. That of course is now; when he stayed with us it wasn't always like that!

One thing that does strike me however is the fact that you do sometimes make allowances for the children in your care, more so than your own at times. Obviously we try and bring our own children up to be caring and sharing, not to steal, or swear, or be disrespectful. My son has been known to say to me on more than one occasion, especially when he was younger, 'You would not have let me get away with that, why should they?' I suppose it's because sometimes you can't blame a child for behaving as they do when you think of the stressful lives they are living. I have always tried to explain to my son as best I can why sometimes I let things go or make allowances for the children. There are certain things they do need to know.

The children of carers, I believe, deserve more appreciation and recognition than we sometimes give them. My son has helped me no end. I'm sure too that he counts his blessings not to have ever been subjected to some of the things these children have had to endure. My son has grown up to be a caring, sensitive lad, always allowing for the teenage hormones kicking in! Not long ago he went to London, for a college test. Not a 'marks out of ten' test, more a personality test to determine what type of work would be best suited to him. It turned out one of the top options was 'social worker'. Well, all I can say is, he's done a lot of the groundwork already.

The young people

The children may be a little apprehensive perhaps at first but they do love to come. We, as support carers, really do get the best of these young people. Because they are also having a break from their family problems, their hang-ups are not with you, therefore you don't get the repercussions that those problems could normally bring. I've had teenagers, maybe one overnight a week or perhaps one weekend a month, and I can honestly say over periods of up to nine months, I haven't ever seen much of the bad behaviour they are renowned for at home. Of course there are times when I do, and this helps when you're relating to parents, offering maybe some advice on how to handle it.

It is not unusual for parents to feel that their children do take notice of us and if we are all sending the same messages, it brings an aspect of consistency into their lives. I remember one boy I cared for, diagnosed as possibly with autism, fourteen years old, lovely happy chappy, always smiling. I looked after him one weekend a month. He was so pleased with himself having taken up footie. His parents had bought him his own football and it went everywhere, I mean everywhere with him. I received a telephone call from his mother who I got on very well with. Her son had blacked her eye with his much-treasured ball, and would I have a word. She wanted back up, support from me. She was obviously distressed, but sharing the problem and having back up in dealing with the situation with her son was so helpful to her. It was easier for her to be firm in telling him off when she knew I would be having something to say about it as well.

Easier said than done however. 'Of course I'll have a word,' I said, but inside I was thinking, what on earth can I do, what am I supposed to say, 'Hi Jack, heard you blacked your mum's eye with your football, try getting the goalpost next time?' Well, all the way over to pick him up I'm facing this task of how do I approach it. For one thing, my son's sitting next to me knowing nothing of this. Out comes Jack to the car, minus the one thing that goes everywhere with him, the football. In the car he gets, we say our hellos. Then I just say, 'Anyway Jack, where's your football? . . . Oh, the police have confiscated it,' he says. 'Whatever for?' I ask, and he says 'I hit my mum in the face with it, that's all'. 'That's all,' my son pipes up (I think we said it together really). 'Oh Jack, you must promise me you'll never do that again,' I say, plus a few words about safety, and taking care of his mum. Apparently, he had been kicking it at the kitchen door just as she was coming out. He did promise to be careful though, and kept his word, he never did it again. I remember my son was laughing about it later on, saying, 'I can't believe he's blacked his mum's eye with a football!' But more astounding to him was the 'That's all' comment, like it was not really a significant enough event to be worth mentioning. Funny? Well, obviously not for his mum.

I must say one of the rewards of this job is undoubtedly the way in which these children keep in touch. I look after young teenagers usually so they are independent and capable enough to make their own way, whereas with younger children, I would think it is less likely to happen. I had a girl ring me from Huddersfield last week that I hadn't heard from in ages. Then I found out that a girl I have recently had placed has a stepbrother who I looked after some time ago, and he wants to come back and see us. It's nice to feel like part of the family.

We do make a change in young people's lives. Sometimes their appreciation shows straight away, sometimes it shows later down the line. As a support carer you need to adapt to each individual child. It's hard work sometimes, but when they still see you as someone who cared about them through a bad stage in their lives, it's wonderful. It's lovely to see them grow – and do they grow – I feel I'm among giants sometimes. I've had some beautiful pictures, letters and cards etc. given and written to me (and even the occasional apology). I treasure them all.

Conclusion

Over the years as a support carer I've looked after forty plus children. I've had hundreds of cuddles, tantrums, and tears. I've had great times, I've despaired and I've worried myself sick. I've made a lot of friends. I've had glimpses of a very different world through their eyes, and I've learned a lot.

By being there, I've helped prevent most of the young people I've looked after from going into long-term care, and I feel privileged to do what I do. It makes me feel good about myself, that I'm part of a set-up that is handing a lifeline to families in crisis.

Chapter 5

Adoption Under Pressure

Tim Earnshaw, Jonathan Helbert and Joy Howard

Introduction

This chapter explores the ideas of Support Care as applied to the specific needs of families who adopt. The setting up of a pilot adoption support project in Bradford is described from the perspectives of the project co-ordinator, the adoptive family's social worker and the support worker to the carers.

Background (Support Care Co-ordinator)

Support Care was developed with the primary aim of preventing family breakdown by offering families in difficulties the support of a part-time foster family. A series of short breaks has been found to relieve tension and help improve relationships within the family. The help and advice offered by Support Carers has been well received by families, and most placements have fulfilled their purpose within six to nine months. Occasionally, a need has been identified for more protracted involvement, and currently the addition of some longer-term provision to our repertoire is under discussion. However, the prime objective remains to keep families together, and children and young people out of the care system (see Chapter 2).

Over the years in Bradford, a number of referrals for a Support Care placement were made by social workers on behalf of adoptive parents. These were seen as families like any other, going through the ups and downs of family life. But were they? In every instance, Support Care was of little help. All of these placements ended in the breakdown of the home situation, and a return to the care system for the child or young person. In every instance, this was a devastating experience for everyone involved. What were the reasons for these negative outcomes?

There were common factors that could be identified. Firstly, it seemed as if the families concerned had left it until things were really desperate before feeling it was acceptable to ask for help. Experience within Support Care has taught us that in the few instances when our efforts have been overtaken by accommodation, the referral had come too late in the day. The earlier the intervention, the more likelihood there is of a successful outcome. An additional commonality was the issue of attachment. Most of the young people involved had had more than one family separation, were understandably reluctant to trust and engage and as a result difficult to love. Most of the adoptive parents had tried and tried again, and were feeling hopeless and worn out. In more than one instance, a child had subsequently been born to the parents, a change of family dynamics that rarely seems to work in favour of the adopted child. In some instances, adoptive placements had been made that were not entirely without reservations both on the part of the placing social worker and the adoptive family – a potential recipe for disaster. Additionally, it was a common experience for adopters that when the going had got tough, the extended family support that had been anticipated tended to melt away, leaving parents isolated and unsupported.

When Jonathan came to me for advice about an adoptive family he was working with, I was not in a position to offer more than short-term intervention; with the experience I had, this did not feel adequate. It seemed to me that what was needed was a family who could stand in for the extended family support that was lacking. A family that could roll with the bad times, and stick with it. A family who could form a caring relationship with the adopted child, help counteract the negatives and build much-needed self-esteem. A family who would be supportive, but not take over. A Support Carer, but in for the long haul, and able to empathise with the very specialised difficulties of a potential adoption breakdown.

I had recently met some new applicants, not yet approved, who immediately sprang to mind as potentially being really well suited to this kind of work. Carole and Simon are a financially comfortable professional couple, with no children of their own. These factors, superficially at any rate, meant that it might prove quite difficult to make matches with our Support Care client group, where the Support Carers' experience of parenting and community base contribute greatly to the success of placements. But these same factors were an indicator of a potentially great match with an adoptive family. From the same social background, and not feeling like a potential challenge as 'expert' parents, it felt as if what could be on offer was a substitute uncle and aunt who could build a sustainable relationship with both child and parents.

Discussions with Simon and Carole began. Their initial enthusiasm for the whole concept of family support remained strong, and the idea of piloting a new scheme within Support Care was also welcomed. We proceeded to a fostering panel approval with a specific match in mind. The placement was duly negotiated and overnight stays began. A detailed account of how things went follows.

The Adopter's perspective (Adoption support worker)

A family in difficulties

I became involved at the point where Bob and Jill (the adoptive parents) contacted the Adoption and Fostering Unit in 2000 requesting help for their son Peter then aged two and a half. He had been placed with them two years earlier when nine months old. The couple had previously adopted a daughter Rachael who, at the time of the referral, was aged seven. Bob and Jill described Peter as an unmanageable child who never seemed to settle and who had developed a range of distressing behaviours such as soiling. The couple had been told by social workers that Peter's mother had used street drugs during her pregnancy and that Peter had shown signs of neonatal abstinence syndrome. However, they had been reassured that Peter was in good health and there should be no concerns over his future development. Bob and Jill's perception of Peter's difficulties was that drugs were still in his system, and in some way affecting him. The couple felt that they had been let down by social services who had placed a 'disabled' child with them despite making clear statements that they did not wish to take such a child. Jill in particular felt saddened that Peter seemed to emotionally avoid her and she had been unable to experience the emotional closeness she had enjoyed when Rachael had been placed. The couple felt nobody had listened to them when they asked for help and experienced a sense of being abandoned by social services. These themes of being let down, abandonment and lack of closeness with the child continue to be a cause of anxiety and distress to the family.

Initial intervention

I co-ordinated a multi-agency response that included a paediatric assessment, the early years education service and the involvement of a child psychologist. A number of practical measures were taken, including Peter starting at a special needs pre-school nursery, and the completion of medical assessments indicating that Peter was in fact in good health. The psychological assessments indicated that Peter was a bright child who learnt quickly. Attempts to encourage the parents to use behavioural strategies met with limited success; it seemed that as the parents developed a response to a particular behaviour so he would develop new behaviours. Working in an adoption support situation was a new experience for those of us involved with Peter and his family. We realised that we needed to pay more attention to the couple's emotional needs and story of 'being let down' and 'abandonment', if we were to maintain the family's confidence and trust. In addition we began to realise that conventional approaches to working with families needed to be modified if they were to be helpful. In 2002, a Registrar on placement at our local Children and Adolescent Mental Health Service reviewed the case, and presented an analysis of Peter's history and difficulties using an attachment model. This provided an alternative story for Peter's parents, giving an explanation for why Peter might be hurtful and provocative towards them, and yet behave well in other settings such as nursery school.

Although a network of service provision had been set in place, 2002 proved to be a very difficult year for the family, with the parents experiencing both health and work difficulties, and with energy levels at a very low ebb. Peter's need to be in control, and to drive a wedge between relationship dyads in the family, was beginning to distress Rachael and led to constant conflict at home. I felt this might be a time when Bob and Jill would call it a day and ask for Peter to be removed. They felt that they needed time away from him but also felt a sense of shame at not being able to manage by themselves. Their family supports were very limited with family members feeling unwilling to have Peter. In the absence of a respite service I negotiated a series of daycare options that proved to be helpful during the school holidays. A mainstream foster carer provided this service. Unfortunately the carer was not available when such a service was requested again, and I was offered some daycare by the foster carer that Peter had lived with when he was a baby. This plan did not materialise either, despite introductory meetings taking place. On reflection, I realised that expecting adopters to accept help from the carer who had first had Peter could be seen as symbolically asking them to acknowledge their failure as adoptive parents. But it was clear that the couple had an ongoing need for respite. Bearing in mind their story of 'being let down' and 'feeling abandoned', what was needed would ideally be a long-term respite arrangement where they would receive a service both during and between crises. Additionally, a long-term arrangement would be more appropriate for Peter who needed to experience continuity of relationships over time. It was at this point, following a discussion with Bob and Jill in early 2003, that a formal request for placement was made to Support Care.

Work with Support Care

Setting up the placement

At the point that I first approached Support Care for advice, in September 2002, Simon and Carole were in the process of being assessed as carers. They sounded promising and I met with Tim, the social worker responsible for their foster carer assessment, and told him about Peter. It was agreed Tim would share anonymised information with the couple. Simon and Carole expressed a strong interest in the family, and felt sympathetic to their situation.

In accordance with fostering practice, Tim acted as link worker for the carer and I was the social worker on behalf of Peter's family. This allowed for both parties to be separately supported and represented if there were difficulties. Support Care had decided with Simon and Carole that they would offer placements for two children each child having a weekend a month. This allowed the couple a 'weekend off' once a fortnight.

We agreed that we would not start the introductory process until the fostering panel had formally approved Simon and Carole as carers. Given that we were planning a long-term respite arrangement, we would follow the same process as one would take when making a planned foster placement. This involved meeting with the prospective carers to brief them. This was followed by a series of meetings at the families' respective homes with agreement that Peter and his parents would visit the carers. Following an informal review attended by all parties, an introduction plan was drawn up, whereby Peter had a day visit that was subsequently followed up by an overnight stay, and another review meeting. Though they were experiencing frustration with the length of time involved in following these procedures, Bob and Jill did feel that the carers took the time to listen to their concerns and got to know Peter.

We have now reached a stage where Peter attends respite on a monthly basis from Saturday through to Sunday. We have regular review meetings on a four monthly basis.

One year in

Bob and Jill had felt frustrated by the long wait, and by an introduction process that seemed cumbersome. They also expressed their view to me that this level of provision was 'too little too late' having waited so long to get a service. However, Bob and Jill are pleased with how things are going now, although there are times when they would wish for more frequent respite. They identify the following as positive aspects of the service:

• The service is regular and reliable.
• The care provided is of high quality and safe.
• The carers respect them as parents and have empathy for their difficulties.

Peter's family did not choose to become service users and their abiding sense is of being let down by social services. Although predictability allows Peter's family to plan 'time off', I think it begins to give them confidence in support services. Being clear about the parameters of the service, and having the delivery of the service structured by social work staff, means that any conflict about the service could be directed *at* staff. The family and the carers are able to get on with the detail of arrangements. There was one point where Simon and Carole were not told the child was taking medication and felt they should have been told. Tim, as their link worker, addressed this at a review saying that as a service provider he felt the carers should have been informed. This was agreed by all.

Simon and Carole take a child-centred approach. Peter enjoys going to stay with them, although he is always pleased to come home again. The parents' views are actively sought, and Bob and Jill are always told about what the carers have been doing with Peter, which helps to promote confidence. The carers are keen to ensure that they praise Peter's achievements, and report back on what he says about his family. Although the carers have learnt that prolonged handovers can distress Peter they make time to talk to the parents on the phone although they are careful not to enter into an 'expert' position by offering advice.

At the time of writing I am at the stage of renegotiating with Peter's parents how other aspects of their adoption support service should be delivered. This is a difficult process, as the early themes of 'letting down' and 'abandonment' resurface and need to be acknowledged. Although we will at some future point need to renegotiate the terms of the respite arrangement, it is interesting that they have not included this in our current conversations. I have the sense that in addition to its practical role the breaks offered by the carers are an important emotional support to the couple and help counter-balance the negative feelings that have been described.

The Carers perspective (Support Care link worker)

Assessment

Carole and Simon initially contacted Bradford's Fostering and Adoption Services in response to a publicity and recruitment campaign highlighting the need for support foster carers. Following an initial interview, the couple attended a foster care preparation group between June and September 2002. This gave the couple an insight into the services being provided to support children and families locally, and confirmed for them that they had something to offer and gain in the field of Support Care.

Carole and Simon's application came to the attention of the Support Care Co-ordinator, Joy Howard, who felt that they could have the potential to consider becoming approved for a pilot project concentrating on Support Care specifically for adoptive families. Joy made an initial contact with them; they were immediately enthusiastic about the idea and were keen to begin the assessment process. Joy was able to commission myself, a former Bradford social worker, who had spent many years in a children and families team, and was now specialising in adoption, to undertake the required home study and present their application to the fostering panel. I also expressed an interest in continuing to act as link worker to the family through their first placement. This enabled the assessment to address the added dimensions that would inevitably come to play in supporting families who were experiencing difficulties with their adopted children. These included developing empathy and sensitivity to the feelings of frustration, disappointment, failure, grief and anger that are associated with adoptive families in crisis.

Throughout the assessment Carole and Simon remained enthusiastic. They were able to explore and challenge their thoughts and feelings, presenting a holistic and non-judgmental view of the task and what they themselves could offer. Both have professional backgrounds, and this was a significant advantage, in that they belonged to the same social milieu as the adopters. They quickly demonstrated an ability to analyse the complex relationships and feelings experienced by the adoptive family and to be clear about the Support Care task and its parameters. Their motivation to become involved, as with most people who consider becoming foster carers, was not financial but more about a wish to put something back into society by 'making a little bit of a difference'. At the time of making their application they also felt they were at a stage in life when they had time to invest in the Scheme, and also that this was a journey, which could lead to a developing relationship with Adoption and Fostering Services, in which they took a strong interest.

Simon and Carole were approved as Support Carers specifically to work alongside adoptive families in early 2003. The fostering panel were impressed, with the couple's ability to demonstrate an understanding of the difficulties that may be experienced by children and parents who were to be supported by the Scheme, and with their potential to undertake the Support Care task.

The placement

Following their approval, Joy convened a meeting with myself, and Jonathan, the adoption social worker who had been supporting Peter's adoptive parents, Jill and Bob. This meeting considered Peter's behaviour and practical care needs and the issues facing both him and the family. We concluded that the offer of Support Care was appropriate and that Carole and Simon had the potential to provide the support. The next stage involved a meeting with Simon and Carole, myself and Jonathan to discuss Peter's individual needs. Emphasis was placed on gaining an understanding of him as an individual, the issues affecting everyone in his family, and establishing clarity about their role in caring for Peter. Time was spent focusing on his current and potential behaviours; in particular an increase in sexualised behaviour and how Carole and Simon would think about and adapt their lifestyle in relation to safe care when he was staying with them. They were given time to consider the match but quickly concluded that they would like to proceed. They felt confident (although a little nervous) that they could offer Peter structure, activities and above all fun, and that they would be able to manage his behaviour appropriately. They were totally in sympathy with Jill and Bob's need for a break.

Jonathan was then in a position to present the adoptive family with information about Simon and Carole to see if they felt comfortable with them as carers for Peter. The next step was for all of the adults involved in the process to meet to plan the purpose and frequency of support and to let the family share more detailed information about the practicalities of caring for Peter. With hindsight, this was possibly the most difficult part of the process. We arranged to meet at the adoptive family's home after the children had gone to bed. Soon after arrival it was clear that emotions were running high and even though Carole and Simon had explored with myself the difficulties that could arise at the meeting, they were not prepared for the outpouring of frustration and anger that had been building over time for the family – clearly they were emotionally and physically 'on the ropes'. This made the meeting uncomfortable for Simon and Carole, being drawn headlong into such highly charged emotions; however the couple look back on the experience as having given them an insight into just how close to breakdown the situation was at the time of them becoming involved. It was also helped by the fact that both have experience of managing difficult meetings in their professional lives. The trigger would appear to have been that the offer of one day of support per month as a starting point was not enough and this prompted an outburst of frustration. Bob and Jill were allowed to vent their feelings, and we were all then able to make progress in covering the ground that was necessary to set up the Support Care plan.

We looked at Peter's needs: behaviour; likes and dislikes; triggers for certain behaviours and strategies the family used to manage difficult behaviour.

We discussed his relationships with parents, sister, family, friends and peers. Behavioural management and progress at school were of particular interest to Carole, as she is a teacher. Peter's health and dietary needs were noted, and both his home routines and special interests were taken on board. The aim throughout was to share all the information that would be needed to enable Carole and Simon to care for Peter in a way that was sympathetic to his needs and to maintain his familiar routines.

We also tried to establish a clear understanding as to the purpose of the support. The adoptive family identified their need for a break from the constant frustration that they were experiencing. They also felt that their daughter Rachael, who resented the fact that attention seemed always to focus on Peter as a result of his 'bad' behaviour, also needed a break from her brother, so that she could spend some positive time with her parents. It was apparent too that the whole family's lifestyle was influenced by the additional stress caused by the long working hours the adoptive couple were having to put into their business.

Frequency and length of the period of involvement are areas where adoption Support Care may differ from traditional Support Care in looking at the potential for a long-term involvement with the child. Experience suggests that careful introductions, and the building up of trusting relationships should be done gradually, and it was important to remain firm in commencing with one day of support per month, to be reviewed and increased to overnight once a month if seen as appropriate, even though the family did not feel that this was enough. Carole and Simon were sympathetic to the couple and were prepared to offer two days per month initially as they felt the couple to be in such turmoil; however it was important to remain firm and not to provide a knee-jerk response. Although not the level of support that they felt they needed, the adoptive parents were able to accept that this was better than nothing.

At Simon and Carole's suggestion we agreed that a good way of introducing the families to each other would be for Jill and Bob to visit at their home for a couple of hours at tea time. The meeting took place the following weekend and proved a success. The family were much less anxious, Peter was able to meet Carole and Simon with his parents present and Rachael was also able to see who was going to be looking after her brother. Peter has been used to being looked after by other people via childminding, relatives, etc. and he did not find it difficult to relate to Carole and Simon as potential carers.

Three initial introductory days were agreed at the planning meeting, and all proceeded according to plan with Peter getting to know Simon and Carole, and visa-versa. Carole and Simon did not experience any major difficulty in caring for Peter. They found that he responded well to clear firm boundaries and although needing occasional reassurance about returning home he soon built up a good relationship with them. Simon and Carole found him to be a bright youngster who enjoyed the attention and the activities that they were able to provide, trips to places of interest and activities in the home such as baking. Peter would on occasions attempt to make difficulties between Carole, Simon and his parents at picking up and dropping off times, but strategies were quickly developed to place the control back with the adults.

At the first review it was possible to share thoughts as to how the visits had been going and the impact on both Peter and the wider family. Simon and Carole were skilful in describing positive aspects of Peter's behaviour while he was with them, without it being perceived as evidence of Bob and Jill 'failing' as parents. The review also considered whether the aims of the support were beginning to be achieved. This will always be a difficult thing to do, as it is hard to separate what is being achieved by the Support Care itself, in relation to other ongoing interventions such as therapy, in the attempt to improve familial relationships. Carole and Simon felt confident to offer monthly overnight stays and all felt that this would be a further benefit in terms of achieving the aims of the placement; to reduce family stress and provide an opportunity for Peter to develop positive relationships. A six month review date was set, although each party was able to convene an earlier review should the need arise.

The visits have gone well. Peter was initially a little anxious about staying overnight but Simon and Carole were able to reassure him and he now takes the visits in his stride, looking forward to both spending the weekend with Carole and Simon, and to going home afterwards. The relationship has the feel of extended family, i.e. aunt and uncle. The last review agreed to maintain the current level of support. Good relationships enable some flexibility in arrangements and although there are occasional glitches in the plans, the structure of support has become stable and manageable.

Reflection

Peter is still living at home with his adoptive family. They are committed to him remaining part of the family and would say that the support that they are being offered by Carole and Simon is an important factor in preventing a breakdown in their ability to care for him. However, long-term issues remain for Peter and his family, which will hopefully be addressed by ongoing therapeutic inputs.

Carole and Simon have found the experience both rewarding, and frustrating. The rewards have been the belief that they are providing a worthwhile service that can offer a young person a positive relationship which develops and promotes their potential. They also believe that such support can reduce the level of crisis and give a family and professionals the opportunity to take stock and attempt to provide the necessary therapeutic input to help the family face the future together.

The frustrations have come, not from the practical task of caring for Peter, but from the wider context of being detached from the therapeutic team that is working with the family. The team's aim is to help Peter develop an appropriate attachment, and for the family to engage in working to improve the quality of relationships for all. It has proved difficult to hold onto the Support Care role when the other professionals involved are apparently not making progress. As the providers of the resource that can enable real work to move forward, it is a frustration if the opportunity is not grasped; it may just be that this will often be the case for Support Carers. There also will be occasions when lack of communication will lead to misunderstandings and tension in the relationship between parents and carers. It is important to address these in a non-blaming way, and part of my role is to act as negotiator to help re-establish calm and restore positive feelings.

Carole and Simon continue to offer Support Care to Peter and his family, and are exploring other possible matches to extend their experience.

Policy context and future developments (adoption support worker)

In December 2000, the Government published its White Paper on adoption (DoH, 2000). This heralded a range of reforms, most significantly that a greater proportion of children would be adopted. In recognition that these children have particular needs a range of Adoption Support measures would be made available. Whilst most aspects of the subsequent Adoption and Children Act 2002 will be implemented in late 2005, the Government, as part of its commitment to adoption, brought the Adoption Support elements of the legislation into force in October 2003. Local Authorities, as part of their Adoption Support planning, are required to ensure that respite services are available and that there is a range of services not only to support but also to *prevent* the breakdown of adoptive placements. In addition, adopters now have a statutory right to have an assessment of their Adoption Support needs, with Local Authorities having a duty to prepare Adoption Support plans. These changes move the idea of respite support in adoption from a marginal to an integral position within the range of Adoption Support services. The recognition of the important role respite can play within Adoption Support has led to responsibility for the embryonic Adoption Support Respite Service being moved from Joy Howard's Support Care scheme to the Adoption and Fostering Unit's Adoption Support Service. We see the key advantages of this move as being that the service is managed by people who have specialist knowledge of the issues raised within adoption support and for the carers. Additionally the service can be directly resourced from within the ring-fenced Adoption Support budget.

At the time of writing we now have four sets of carers offering placements for up to eight children. These carers are being supported by a permanent, dedicated, social work post. We now know from a recent survey of local adopters that there are experienced adoptive families offering their time and skills to help support other adoptive families. We plan in the future to look towards this group of people as potential carers.

Conclusion

This account has demonstrated one way in which the ideas of Support Care can be successfully adapted to accommodate the specific needs of individual families. It is an example of what can be achieved by thinking 'outside the box' – being alert to possibilities, and open to innovation. There will undoubtedly be expansion of the new adoption support scheme, which will hopefully also inspire and share practice issues with similar developments in other organisations. The only caveat to be entered is to be mindful of the need for government to be similarly proactive in offering support to all families in difficulties, so that birth parents do not retrospectively feel disadvantaged in comparison with the families who have taken on the care of their children through adoption.

References

DoH (2000) *Adoption, a New Approach*. White Paper. London: The Stationery Office.

Further reading

DoH (2003) *Adoption Support Services Guidance to Accompany the Adoption Support Services (Local Authorities) (England) Regulations 2003*. London: DoH.

Department of Education and Skills (2004) *Draft Adoption Regulations and Guidance for Consultation: Adoption Support and Adoption Support Agencies*. London: DfES.

Fahlberg, V. (1994) *A Child's Journey through Placement*. London: BAAF.

Lowe, N. and Murch, M. (1999) *Supporting Adoption: Reframing the Approach*. London: BAAF.

Chapter 6

Keeping it Local

Sue Smith

Introduction

In this chapter I describe how Birmingham's Neighbourhood Care Service began and how it has developed and expanded over time. I will be exploring:
- The background to the current service.
- Funding issues.
- How it fits in with current legislation.
- Our successes.
- Some of the pitfalls and lessons we have learnt.

I have drawn data from government publications, our own records, case studies and evaluation forms.

The chapter is not intended as a blueprint for providing Support Care but rather as a means of raising awareness about an effective, and often overlooked, placement option for children and young people.

Background

In 1989 Birmingham had a flourishing sponsored childminding scheme, which offered free daycare to families of under-fives experiencing parenting difficulties. The service was popular with the families who used it, to gain a welcome break from daily childcare, but the feedback from the childminders who provided the service was that it would be much more effective if it offered more than just 'nine to five'. Many families who used the service had told childminders that they often found they could cope during the day but they found evenings and weekends the hardest times. With this in mind it was decided to test a pilot service that would offer more flexibility, to include evening, weekend and overnight placements.

The three-year pilot was named 'Neighbourhood Care' because even at that early stage it was recognised that the most effective way of delivering a service to under-fives was to keep it local, thus giving families the opportunity to maintain responsibility for attending placements without the need for additional intervention. In much the same way working parents organise their own childcare.

In setting up the service we consulted closely with families, and used the information we gathered to shape the service. The same comments came up time and time again, and they were along the lines of:

When I ask for help I don't want to wait for ages before I get It.

I need a placement that suits our needs not yours.

I don't want everyone to know that I can't look after my kids.

We also consulted with area social work teams in order to determine geographically which were the areas of greatest need.

The remit was to recruit twelve families, where one member was already a registered childminder, who would offer placements to children from outer-city estates in South Birmingham. These estates had been targeted because mortality rates amongst the under thirty-fives and unemployment rates were both higher than the national average. There were also a disproportionate number of single parents and requests for reception into care from the identified estates.

By September 1989 we had approved fifteen carers based in, or within easy travelling distance of, the identified geographical target areas. Referrals were taken from social workers, health visitors, hospital and mental health teams, family support units, family centres and GPs. It was envisaged that the scheme would provide a service for thirty children per year in order to prevent family breakdown. In fact the scheme placed ninety-four children in the first year and it didn't become operational until September. In the first full year we placed one hundred and thirty-six children. The demand was phenomenal and ensured that the pilot was such a success that we were included in mainstream funding in April 1992.

Just as we began to evaluate the service Birmingham Social Services implemented the Children Act 1989 and turned everything upside down. We took advice from our legal department and it soon became clear that we would have to make a number of changes to the scheme. Most importantly our age limit was raised from five to eight, which increased the number of referrals to an already overstretched system. The main impact was that children who stayed overnight were now defined as 'accommodated', had a knock on effect.

Under the old boarding out regulations (DoH, 1988) a child could stay with a carer for anything up to seven nights without being classed as 'in care'. However, the Children Act stated that any child who stayed in a placement, funded by the local authority, for longer than 24 hours would be classed as a child in local authority care or 'accommodated' and would be subject to Looked after Children (LAC) procedures.

So how did this affect the Neighbourhood Care scheme?
- All carers had to be assessed and approved at fostering panel as foster carers.
- Each overnight placement was subject to the completion of governmental 'looked after children' (LAC) paperwork.

We came to an agreement that a fostering panel would approve our carers as 'foster carers for the Neighbourhood Care scheme' only. However, it was the paperwork that was associated with foster placements that created the greatest number of problems initially. Foster carers were assessed using a standard format as laid out in an assessment tool known as 'Form F' (BAAF, 1991). Many of the issues raised in the Form F assessment were irrelevant to short term Support Care and many other more relevant skills overlooked. It was eventually agreed that we could complete our assessments using a modified Form F tailored to the needs of our service.

The statutory paperwork relating to the child's placement proved more problematic. To ensure that the needs of a child in foster care were met the child's social worker was required to complete several forms to ensure that the foster carer had all the relevant information necessary to care for the child. Because of the nature of foster placements, this included detailed information about the child's medical and educational needs, and the local authority's plan for the child during placement. Whilst some of this information was essential to the welfare of a child, for our service much of it was not. Eventually we came to an agreement that only part of the paperwork needed for Looked after Children would be required for children using Neighbourhood Care.

The greatest stumbling block proved to be the statutory medical requirements. Every child entering foster care is expected to have a full medical examination. This is to identify and address any medical needs that may have been overlooked but also to protect the foster carer from allegations of abuse. To be effective the examination should take place at the start of every placement. Unfortunately in a series of short placements this is impractical and so after the first period of support the medical is rendered ineffective. However the examination was a statutory requirement and we could find no way around this. As can be imagined parents were confused by the mixed messages they were receiving. On the one hand they were told that their children were to be placed with a local childminder who could offer extra care in terms of evenings, weekends and overnights. The service would be flexible and easy to access; they would retain parental responsibility and should feel no stigma attached to the placement. On the other hand we then confronted them with a large amount of official paperwork to sign and expected them to take their child to their GP for a medical, clutching a form which clearly said that they were in the care of the Local Authority.

Referrals for overnight places, which had previously been made by a number of referring agencies, now had to be directed to the child's social worker for the completion of the necessary paperwork. This increased the workload of the social workers involved who were not exactly delighted to be asked to complete up to three separate and lengthy pieces of paperwork per child for a service, which they had previously accessed through a referral form. Four carers left the scheme when they knew that they would be expected to take part in a detailed assessment on them for a role which they had successfully fulfilled for two years.

It is probably a testament to how the service is valued, and needed, that we managed to get through these problems. After operating the service within these procedures for ten years, recent changes in legislation have enabled us to leave the fostering service and return full circle to recruiting and using childminders rather than foster carers.

How does Support Care fit with current legislation?

The Neighbourhood Care Team has had experience of placing children with both foster carers and childminders. Essentially, in terms of the service we deliver and the impact on the families who use it, there is little difference. Support Care does not fit comfortably within any existing legislation. We have made placements under both Section 20 and Section 17 of the Children Act 1989 and both require 'tweaking' in order to fulfil legal requirements and remain safe and operable. For many years the service provided placements with foster carers under Section 20 of the Children Act 1989 as previously described. Section 20 was the section that covered voluntary accommodation: in other words, children were placed with the consent of the parents. In order to do this effectively we had to modify the assessment process. We didn't address areas such as loss and moving children on to permanency but instead included sections on working with parents and social inclusion. When arranging placements we also used a modified version of the LAC paperwork, including the medical examination.

The **disadvantages** of Section 20 placements are:

- The paperwork doesn't fit the task.
- The medical is intrusive and ultimately ineffective unless it is undertaken before each period of Support Care. This would mean a child who stays with a carer for six weekends would need six medicals.
- If the placements are recorded under LAC procedures this artificially inflates the figures when most local authorities are seeking to do the opposite.

- The review process does not fit with Support Care placements. By the time the first review is due to take place, often the placement is finished.
- If the service is not using existing foster carers the assessment and approval process is a lengthy one even when using a modified version. This can adversely impact on recruitment.
- Not all professionals can complete LAC paperwork, which limits referrals for overnight placements to social work teams.
- Families are sometimes put off accessing the service when they realise that the process is similar to foster care because they fear the stigma.

The **advantages** of Section 20 placements are:
- It enables local authorities to retain the services of experienced foster carers who might otherwise leave the department.
- Children and young people are safeguarded within the placement.
- The fostering standards and regulations ensure that placements are effectively monitored.

In November 2002, the Adoption and Children Act 2002 received Royal Assent and amended the Children Act 1989 to enable local authorities to accommodate children under Section 17 for up to 28 consecutive nights. Section 17 (provision of services for children in need, their families and others) of the Children Act 1989 now allows the accommodation of children provided that the initial assessment of the child's needs shows that:
- There being no person who has parental responsibility for him.
- His being lost or abandoned.
- The person who has been caring for him being prevented (whether or not permanently, and for whatever reason) from providing him with suitable accommodation and or care.

(The Adoption and Children Act, 2002)

The Neighbourhood Care Team has used this change in legislation to remove our provision of Support Care from our Fostering Services to Family Support by recruiting childminders. Childminders who are able to provide overnight care are approved and regulated by Ofsted, using fourteen national standards to ensure quality care (DfES, 2003). In addition to this, because we are providing placements for children in need, we have also added our own procedures and protocols for Support Care which includes an additional assessment, a family placement meeting, a Support Care plan, a contract, monthly supervision, training and an allocated support worker.

The **disadvantages** of Section 17 placements with childminders are:
- The legislation does not call for any additional safeguards when placing children in need. Childminders' only legal requirement is to comply with the fourteen standards when caring for all the children. Unlike fostering there is no requirement to review or monitor placements.

- Without statutory reviews the placement may drift if not carefully co-ordinated and monitored.
- The approval process for childminders is not as thorough as that for foster carers.
- The onus is on childminders to regulate themselves using the childminding standards (DfES, 2003).

The **advantages** of Section 17 placements with childminders are:
- In order to become registered Ofsted expects potential childminders to undertake initial training including a paediatric first aid certificate, Criminal Records Bureau checks on all members of the family over sixteen, a health and safety check on their home and an examination by their GP if any health issues are identified. Although this is not as thorough as fostering approval it is an effective starting point for new Support Carers.
- There is no barrier to including additional safeguards to the existing requirements. This makes it much easier to tailor the service to meet the requirements of Support Care placements. Trying to achieve the same outcome by cutting down or modifying existing fostering requirements can prove much more difficult with many authorities reluctant to take the risk.
- Placements with childminders carry no stigma. The paperwork involved is not linked to foster care. Families who use the service are reassured that the placement is not a precursor to accommodation.
- Childminders are often ideally placed within their local community to help direct families to local services and assist social integration.
- Because the only statutory paperwork we require is the Department of Health Initial Assessment (DoH, 2000) we can take referrals from a variety of professionals including health visitors, midwives and Sure Start outreach workers.

Another important development was the Government's proposals as laid out in the Green paper *Every Child Matters* (HM Treasury, 2003). These proposals have been invaluable in focusing attention, and funding, on the importance of early preventative action, including targeted and specialist support, and a variety of placement options which support families to enable children to fulfil their potential. As Young People and Families' Minister, Margaret Hodge, said at the time of the consultation process:

Child protection cannot be separated from policies to improve children's lives more widely. We want to reform children's services to best protect children from risk of harm. At the same time, we want to shift the balance to prevention by providing greater support to all families.

(www.dfes.gov.uk/speeches)

For a long time, family support and preventative work has been seen as the 'soft' end of social work; and families needing such a service have found themselves competing for resources with interventions of much higher profile, like child protection. Overstretched social work teams often focus of necessity on crisis management, and have little time for early preventative work even if they appreciate the long-term benefits. However, as family support and prevention gain a higher profile and attract additional funding, so the ability to provide these services has increased. Our own service has seen the benefit of this when, in 2001, we received two years funding from the Government's *Quality Protects* programme. One of the objectives of this programme was to promote a variety of placement options for children in need. This money was the first step in allowing us to expand and develop the service.

Why does Support Care work?

Support Care doesn't work for everyone. Occasionally placements are requested when they are too late to be effective and negative patterns of behaviour have become so deeply ingrained in families that it is difficult to prevent family breakdown. Occasionally families are directed to Support Care because it is easier to access than other services but it may not be the service they have requested, and occasionally the family home is just too dangerous for the child to remain there. However, for the vast majority of families who are referred to us Support Care is seen as one of the most effective and valued services they use.

Families are referred to us for a number of reasons but our experience is that many of the families requesting the service are socially isolated and living on benefits or low incomes. The support networks that many of us take for granted don't exist for them. Without the support of family and friends and the opportunity to take a break from time to time the role of parent can quickly become overwhelming. These feelings can lead to depression, and sometimes to alcohol and substance misuse, which further aggravate the situation. If the parents in question have also had a poor or damaging experience of parenting themselves then they have fewer inner resources to call on, and family relationships can quickly deteriorate.

Families are often reluctant to ask for help for a number of reasons. If they have had an unhappy experience of support services in the past, they may feel that they will not be taken seriously, or alternatively may be taken *too* seriously, and their children may be removed.

The following key points are some of the reasons why Support Care is seen so positively by the families who use it:

- Families, children and young people have indicated to us, both verbally, and through our evaluation forms, that they feel that they are listened to and are part of the placement process.
- Placements are tailored to the family's needs.

- Placements are time-limited and contractual. Both families and carers know exactly where they stand.
- There is a fast, flexible response.
- There is no stigma attached.
- The carer's initial training emphasises the need to work with parents to promote social integration.

Often very short periods of support are enough to diffuse the tension within families. Many of the problems that families are experiencing are put in proportion by sharing them with a sympathetic listener who is able to point them towards other specialist services. This often means that families enter into a more effective working relationship with other professionals. When responded to promptly, many families have found that as little as six weekends has been enough to provide valuable 'time out' which prevents an escalation of the difficulties they are experiencing. This is often enough to prevent family breakdown.

What lessons have we learnt?

That we should listen to what families are saying to us, is one lesson. There is a view that parents will abuse the service if they have too great a voice in the decision-making process, but often families only misuse a service that they feel has been imposed on them. In our experience if they are responded to promptly, and feel part of the referral and placement process, families' requests for support are often more modest and reasonable than expected. However, unless families self-refer, it can be difficult to ensure the prompt response and democratic decision-making in the early stages of the referral. This is always dependent on the pressures on the referring agency. For this reason another valuable lesson we have learnt is that the service is most effectively delivered by taking referrals from a variety of professional agencies working with the family rather than increasing the pressure on just one source.

Until recently this type of service was given low priority when budgets were allocated. Many similar schemes across the country have had their funding cut or withdrawn when priority was given to other services. Local authorities may see the benefits of preventative family support but struggle to identify funding to set up and maintain their own scheme. Historically the focus for funding tends to be on child protection, and maintaining existing placements for Looked after Children, with very little left over for new initiatives.

Before allocating finances many authorities would want evidence that the service would reduce the LAC figures. The failure to do this is often the reason behind refusal to increase and develop the service or the withdrawal of funding all together. This is compounded by the difficulty in producing 'hard' data to support the anecdotal feedback that Support Care prevents a number of children from entering the care system.

Our own experience was that after the initial interest in our successful pilot the service was continually overlooked and denied adequate funding to enable it to expand and develop. Indeed, for over eight years the service survived on a 'shoestring' budget and with only the support of the referring agencies. The lesson learnt is that even though the current climate is more conducive to providing Support Care these types of services are still very fragile and will remain so until firmly embedded in legislation and social policy.

Finally, experience has shown us the importance of adequate support and training for our carers. Support Care offers a unique role for carers to work with parents as para-professionals providing an advice, support and information service to allow families to access other services themselves, when the placement ends. In order for carers to fulfil this role we have found that it is important to tailor our training to meet the specific requirements of this type of care and not confuse it with the skills needed for either childminding or foster care.

The advantages of a local service

Social isolation is often one of the main factors in the request for Support Care. The inability to call on family or friends for help and support when times get difficult can lead to even the smallest issues escalating into crisis. The single, most immediately effective, support we can offer families is the opportunity to take a break from the tensions within the family to allow them space to decide the way forward themselves. However, Support Care is most productive as part of a package of support which enables the family to move on when the placement ends. Without this opportunity some families may come to the end of the placement finding that little has changed and may eventually slip back into familiar negative patterns of behaviour.

Support Carers have a valuable role in helping families to find other solutions. Outside of the need for specialist professional services, the Support Carer can offer invaluable advice on childcare, coping strategies and direct the family to other local services. This is especially important for families with young children who may find it too daunting to access local groups such as playgroups, mother and toddler groups, or Sure Start. Neighbourhood carers are childminders and as such are firmly embedded in their local community. They can help integrate families with young children back into that community and can support young people to become involved in local initiatives. Many of our carers live in the same areas as the families we refer to them. They have often had similar experiences and are less intimidating than other professionals who may be involved with the family.

As one mother said about one of our carers:
She's just another mum, she doesn't look down her nose at me. She's seen it all so I can tell her anything, nothing fazes her, asking her stuff isn't a big deal like it is talking to my social worker. She always has an idea for something to try. Sometimes I can't be bothered but I know its good advice and sometimes I try it. It's nice to know she's there.

This is from a single grandmother caring for three young children:
It was great to have a break and I was dreading it coming to an end but she just said that I should come to playgroup with her one day and meet everyone. I can't believe how nervous I was, I'd tried to go when I first had the kids but it was so cliquey and I hated it. I couldn't think what to say and they just ignored me after a bit. It was different going with her though, everyone knew her and because I was with her I was accepted straight away. I knew if I went on my own I would bump into her sometimes and then after a bit it didn't matter if she was there or not. I still go now with the little one and I've even made a couple of friends.

For families with young children local placements provide an opportunity to have the same experience of childcare as families who are able to pay for and choose their own. Young children are reassured by staying in a familiar area and the responsibility for taking and collecting the children to and from the placement remains with the family.

In some circumstances it may be better to place the child outside their local area, if they are to be protected from someone with whom contact is restricted for instance. Older children and young people may also benefit from breaking links and patterns of anti-social behaviour in their area for a short while. In our experience, however, in the majority of cases, families with young children are best served by a service that allows them the same choices and opportunities in placements that those of us with friends, family or regular income take for granted.

Multi-agency and partnership working

Support Care provides ideal opportunities for multi-agency and partnership working. We entered into a two-year partnership with the Birmingham Sure Start mainstream programme, which enabled us to develop and expand the service by providing publicity and recruitment materials, training facilities and additional placements. In turn we were able to help with Sure Start targets such as local employment, promoting children's health and educational needs within the placement, and providing a service to vulnerable families who lived outside the Sure Start programme boundaries. We also intend to use funding from the Heart of Birmingham Primary Care Trust to expand the service in that part of the city.

Many voluntary agencies such as Barnardo's and the Children's Society are often also willing to pilot or promote Support Care schemes in partnership with a local authority or through their role as lead body in Sure Start programmes. The change to Section 17 placements (The Adoption and Children Act 2002) has enabled us to take referrals from a wider variety of professionals working with the family and in some cases the only involvement a family will have with social services is through Neighbourhood Care. Neighbourhood Care takes referrals from health visitors, Sure Start outreach workers, midwives, GPs and teachers. Referrals without the involvement of a social worker are only successful if the needs of the family are met solely through the placement. This tends to be where family tensions have been identified early, and a small amount of support is enough to prevent an escalation into a crisis. In families with complex problems, and a number of issues that need to be addressed in conjunction with the placement, or in child protection cases, social worker involvement is essential. By accepting referrals from other professionals, we have found that we are able to reach many families much earlier than we would have done if we had waited until they came to the attention of social services.

Family placement meetings

One important factor in the success or failure of the placement is the expectations of the parents and young people who use the service. We have found that the best way to ensure that everyone has a clear understanding of the purpose of the placement is to hold a family placement meeting in the carer's home.

When a referral is made we receive a placement request attached to the child or young person's initial assessment. The Department of Health's Initial Assessment Record (DoH, 2000) is undertaken for each child using the service. This document is a tool, which allows referrers to make a comprehensive assessment of the child's needs, and covers areas such as emotional and social development, health, education, family relationships, and strengths and limits of parenting capacity. We then use this information to match the child or young person to a suitable carer. When a match has been made we encourage families to visit the carer informally before the family placement meeting takes place. The informal visit allows families the opportunity to decide if they are happy with our choice of a placement and makes the more formal family placement meeting less intimidating. When very young children are involved it also gives parents the opportunity to decide whether the visit or the meeting are the most suitable opportunities for them to meet the carer.

The family placement meeting is attended by the family, the carer, the referrer and the Neighbourhood Care support worker. The meeting is a forum for everyone involved in the placement process to come together and decide what package of support would be most beneficial to the family. The meeting is also an opportunity to complete the Neighbourhood Care plan and contract. Everyone involved in the placement process has a copy of these forms, which avoids confusion about dates, times and the needs of the children, and promotes openness and partnership.

We have found that the most effective way of ensuring that the placement runs smoothly is to be clear from the outset about individual responsibility, expected outcomes and any other key tasks which need to be undertaken with the family in order to help them to move on when the placement ends. The family placement meeting is the ideal forum for this to take place.

Comments from families and referring agencies

The following quotes are some of the comments from families and referring agencies which we have collected on our evaluation forms:

For many families, when things go wrong it is a huge benefit, and often one of the most significantly helpful supports to the family, to be able to refer children to the Neighbourhood Care service.

Health visitor

Excellent. Enables a quick, flexible response. A real practical support to families with young children.

Duty worker on a children and families team

The only stability in our lives at the moment has been the help yourselves and the carer have given us . . . The scheme has helped the children in so many ways I could not start to tell you, only that the care and stability the children have received has been invaluable.

Gemma, a single parent with two children

I was a little bit scared of leaving my children and what would be thought of me but everyone was so nice and they know so much about what children need and they were kind to me.

Nighat, a young mother with five children

The carer was a great person and my son couldn't wait to get there. It made me see that she wasn't doing anything special, just giving him some time, and not being so hard on him, like me, and I could do that too, and I did, and now we get on better. Thank you.

Chanel, a single parent aged 17 with one child

I couldn't suggest any improvements to the service. You seem to have thought of everything! So just lots more of it please.

A social worker

Families find this service very useful. It provides time out and gives us space to work with them on other matters.

Sure Start outreach worker

I was very impressed by the prompt response, which made all the difference to the family who were very cynical about the possibility of a placement. This is a very professional well-organised service.

Duty social worker

Thank you, thank you, thank you. You've saved our lives. I'm going to tell everyone about you.

Julie, mother of three children under five

Case studies

Jatinder

Jatinder was a young Bangladeshi woman living in a hostel with five-month-old twins and a three-year-old daughter. Jatinder had no family in this country, and had been rejected by her husband's family, and the community, because she had reported her husband for domestic violence. She spoke very little English and was finding caring for the children in a limited space very difficult. All the other residents were white or African/Caribbean; Jatinder was unable to hold a conversation with them and had made no friends. She was feeling very depressed and anxious about the future.

Jatinder's GP and Health Visitor were concerned about the delays in re-housing Jatinder and her possible rejection of the twins because of her depression. The Health Visitor referred the twins to our service for daycare and one weekend a month for six months. Although we had a carer living nearby we felt that Jatinder would benefit from a placement with a carer who could speak the same language and had links with the Asian community. Jatinder was placed with Bushra, a Pakastani carer with three teenage children. Bushra lived in a predominantly Asian area in a part of the city that was some distance from Jatinder's original home, so avoiding harassment. In addition to the respite offered by the placement Bushra was able to help Jatinder re-integrate into the community by introducing her to other young mothers in the area. At the end of the placement Jatinder had been re-housed in an area not far from Bushra. She was able to build on the links and friendships she had made during the placement and still valued Bushra as a source of advice. The accommodation was not ideal and Jatinder was still living on a low income but she was less isolated and feeling more positive about the future. She had registered her daughter at the local school and had joined a local stay-and-play group run by Bangladeshi women. Jatinder was attending English classes through Sure Start and was keen to get involved, by helping in her daughter's school when she started.

Donna

Donna, was a white English single parent in her late twenties, with two sons aged five and two. Donna was suffering from severe postnatal depression, which had never been treated. She had completely rejected her two-year-old son and he was treated as a scapegoat for everything that went wrong in the family. Donna's negative feelings and comments about him had also influenced the way her elder son related to his brother. Her two-year-old son, not surprisingly, exhibited extreme attention-seeking behaviour which reinforced the view that he was 'the naughty one'. Donna was referred to Neighbourhood Care by her social worker but was very reluctant to use the service. She said she 'wasn't prepared to be judged by another mother' and when she discovered that the service was delivered through social services she was afraid of the stigma, and the possibility that her children would not be returned to her at the end of the placement.

Donna reluctantly agreed to visit Maggie, a Neighbourhood Carer. At the initial visit Donna was very distressed. She was sobbing and unkempt, as were both the children. After lots of reassurance, and consultation with Donna, it was agreed that the children would spend one weekend in every three with Donna, and initially her two-year-old son would receive full daycare for six weeks. This would then become three days per week until the end of the placement. She was also referred to the local Family Service Unit for family therapy.

Donna told Maggie that she spent the whole of the first weekend, when the children were in placement, sleeping. During the following week she visited her GP who prescribed anti-depressants. Gradually over a number of weeks Donna began to feel that she was taking control of her life again. She developed a strong supportive relationship with Maggie and was reassured by the success of the behaviour management techniques the carer passed on to her. She also began to see that her young son's behaviour was not 'naughty' but just appropriate to his age and needs. She saw his behaviour improve as she began to respond to him warmly and in an age-appropriate way.

At the end of the placement Donna became very anxious about her ability to cope without the service and an extension was put in place to allow her to explore further some options for the future. In total the placement lasted eight months. In that time Donna dealt with her postnatal depression and her relationship with her son. She joined a local slimming group where she lost weight and made friends whom she began to socialise with. She also enrolled at college on a computer studies course that provided a crèche place for her son.

When Maggie met Donna three months after the placement ended Donna said, 'The day I came to visit your house was the day my life changed. After that we started to become a normal family'. Donna was still enjoying her course and was looking forward to getting a job at the end of it.

The future

Over the past two years the service has gone from strength to strength. Birmingham's Social Care and Health Directorate has committed to a planned expansion of the service over four years. From 2002 to 2004 we expanded the existing service in South Birmingham and employed two support workers and a team assistant to take the development forward. We have revised the referral and placement procedure in the light of the change to Section 17 placements (The Adoption and Children Act 2002), and with the help of the Sure Start funding, we were able to prepare new promotional and information leaflets, and to develop our in-house training programme. We have increased the carers' pay and still been able to remain a cost-effective service. During this year we are rolling the service out into the Heart of Birmingham and have so far been successful in recruiting three new carers in this area. During next year the service will finally become city-wide. It is estimated that within three years the number of children placed annually will increase from one hundred to six hundred. In addition to the development of the under-eights service we are currently working with targeted family support teams to pilot a Support Care service for young people aged nine to fourteen, and the support worker responsible for the nine-plus service has been successfully recruiting carers. The service currently has fifteen carers for the under eights and five carers for the nine-to-fourteen age group. We have capacity for thirty-four carers overall, and we hope to achieve this target within twelve months.

Funding can be a stumbling block when local authorities consider developing a Support Care service. While no one can deny that early preventative work with families is effective, many authorities find it difficult to justify the necessary costs if the results are not immediate; so priority continues to be given to child protection and maintaining existing foster placements. Support Care demands a change of attitude towards prevention. Thinking has to be long term. It will be difficult to evidence a reduction in accommodation statistics in the short term and an evaluation based on this alone is unproductive. Anecdotally, it is clear that Support Care relieves family tension and prevents family breakdown; and equally importantly improves the quality of life for the families who use it. A successful Support Care service will help to address the balance between early intervention and 'fire fighting'.

There has never been a better time to start a Support Care service. Preventative family support is on the Government's agenda, and the Fostering Network has begun a three-year project to promote and support the development of such schemes nation-wide.

It is interesting to note that a family of three can currently receive eight weekends of Neighbourhood Care for less than the cost of a week in an external foster placement; and those eight weekends may be all that is needed to prevent that family entering the care system.

References

BAAF (1991) *Form F: Information on Prospective Substitute Parent(s)*. London: BAAF.

DfES (2003) *Day Care and Child Minding (National Standards) (England) Regulations*. London: The Stationery Office.

DoH (1988) *The Boarding-out of Children (Foster Placement) Regulations. Statutory Instrument 2184*. London: HMSO.

DoH (2000) *Framework for the Assessment of Children in Need and their Families*. London: The Stationery Office.

HM Treasury (2003) *Every Child Matters*. London: The Stationery Office www.dfes.gov.uk/speeches

Chapter 7

Have You Tried This?

Wanda Collins

Introduction

In this chapter, I write as a neighbourhood carer with the Birmingham's Neighbourhood Care Scheme; and share my experiences, and give my views, on Support Care.

When I left school, I trained in childcare. I met my husband, got married, had four children and decided to care for other peoples' children in our home, at the same time as bringing up our own children. We both became Registered Childminders. Twelve years ago we registered with Birmingham's Neighbourhood Care Service. Neighbourhood Care developed as a family support service for families with children aged up to eight, using foster carers to offer short-term, part-time support to families. Neighbourhood Carers live in the local community and can provide a range of placement options, from day care to overnight and weekend care. The placements are flexible, time limited and planned, and are individually tailored to meet the needs of each family. The aims are to:

- Support families to enable children to stay at home.
- Give families a breathing space.
- Support the child's health and education needs in the placement.
- Help families to make links in the local community.

Since becoming Neighbourhood Carers our feet haven't touched the ground, life couldn't be busier, never a dull moment; it is interesting, challenging and of course, rewarding. I have met and have worked with so many people, from parents and their children and relations, to local schools, playgroups, community centres through health visitors, social workers, to name but a few.

My role is to support parents and help look after their children. The specific needs of the family are paramount to their placement; and understanding, listening and being sympathetic with parents is essential and of course, giving them time – time to talk. Parents talk openly about their problems which sometimes, they won't tell people in authority. As a parent, I feel that I can relate to their problems, their children and family life in an understanding way, especially when I tell them that I too had problems with my children, they weren't the easiest to look after, and by using that experience this can help other parents.

Sometimes parents bring their children and all they can see are the negative things about them. By saying that they can't cope, they feel depressed because they feel they are no good at being a parent. I have explained that children of a certain age may go through patches of unreasonable behaviour, which can be difficult to cope with. When the parents come to collect their children they have the opportunity to see their child playing with other children. Sometimes they have been amazed, seeing their child actually playing and sharing toys with other children. They may not have ever had the opportunity to witness this before. Parents see a positive and loving side of their child.

With a regular respite care plan, the parents can see a change in their child and have a more positive attitude to their children. The children seem to enjoy being with other children and conforming to regularity and a daily routine of activities, rather than not having structure to the day. I explain to the children what we are going to do during the day, so they know what to expect and they can request to do things they may want to do. So we fit in what they want to do, within reason; for example, making a card or going to the park.

Case Study 1

The children who come may have their own specific needs: one mother was at her wits end with her son who had Asperger's Syndrome and was absolutely obsessed with trains. She had bought every train she could find but nothing was new to him. She felt that she needed a break from him. He came on a regular Saturday daytime placement. I gained his confidence and took him on the train to the airport. We watched the aeroplanes taking off and come in to land; I bought him a simple model of an aeroplane. When we got back from this trip, it must have triggered his interest, as he wanted aeroplanes to play with. His Mum was over the moon. It was coming up to Christmas and a lot of anxieties were over, she could relax a bit, she could start buying for his new interest – and I felt as though this placement had worked and been beneficial to both mother and child.

Case Study 2

Another example of success was when two school children had come for the weekend bringing a teddy from school with its briefcase of possessions and its own diary. It was a project from school: teddy had to spend the weekend with the child who then must write about it in the diary. The teddy and children did exciting things together; compared paw prints with handprints, and wrote about their adventures in the book. The children were pleased they had done their homework whilst in my care. When I took the children home and the children showed their mother what they had done, she burst into tears. Apparently the school took great delight in always 'having a go' at the mother for not responding to letters coming from the school. What they did not know was that she was illiterate; and they probably would have belittled her again if the teddy had returned without a contribution in the class book. She was so very happy to have had that support, it made her feel great; later she went on a literacy course as she had gained that confidence, and sent me a thank-you card which she had specially written. This is when I feel as though being on the scheme will have made a difference to a child's whole family.

Case Study 3

One evening, the doorbell rang and an eight-year-old boy, whom we had looked after, was sitting on the doorstep clutching a bag. He told me that he didn't want to be at home and had come to my house to live. I invited him in, and gave him a drink, whilst I rang his mother to say where he was. She said they had had an argument, and he had sneaked out of the house. We were just about to play a board game so he joined in. Halfway through the game, which he was losing badly, he got up and said he had to get back home as his mom would be worried about him. That was one way of sending him back home! When the boy got back home, his mum rang and said he had apologised to her on his return. She was happy to know he had come to our house, as he was safe.

Families who I have worked with, will always say 'hello', even though no one else around will know how we know each other, as that time of help was in the past. It is a situation of respect from both sides, as that parent appreciates what I had done, but also I feel honoured that I had been asked to be involved as their foster carer, and that they trusted me. At Christmas, we receive lots of cards from families who have been with us from the Neighbourhood Care Service. It is a lifeline for families in a crisis situation.

Case Study 4

One night, movement could be heard from the children's bedroom. I went in expecting to see someone awake through the dim light of the landing; but all eyes were closed. I put my hand onto the duvet cover to cover one of the children when I felt something cold and wet. I jumped back with fright and reached for the bedroom light, as I didn't know what I had felt. To my amazement the goldfish was on the bed and not in its bowl; it was soon revived and back in water, but it gave me such a shock. The little boy, who had it, said he wanted to sleep with it: good job I went in when I did! The following day we arranged to go to the Sea Life Centre and bought him a special Nemo fish to take to bed instead.

Case Study 5

Fostering has taught me a lot. One Christmas, my two daughters each had a very expensive walking, talking, doll. At the time, I thought that by giving such a special present to them would make up for all the times which they had shared their toys with other children in our care. The following day, a little girl Katie came, and I advised my daughters to put their best dolls upstairs so they didn't get broken and to keep them as their own special present. My daughter would not and objected, saying, 'But I want Katie to play with it'. I replied, 'But it's your best Christmas present and you'll be upset if it breaks'. She argued, 'I want Katie to play with it to see what my doll does'. I walked away and left the children playing with the doll, and I felt ashamed of myself. All these years I had taught my children to share toys, to play and look after the other children, and it was I who was being the selfish one, all I thought about was how much I had paid for the dolls. I felt proud of my daughter, and I felt so guilty of my attitude. Fostering does teach us things even as adults.

Reflections on my experience as a Support Carer

When I am helping children survive trauma, which they have either been through themselves, or watched in others, is the time when I need to be at my most thoughtful and sensitive. How do you comfort a child who has just witnessed a traumatic experience, yet thought it was great being in a police car with the siren on? It is situations like that which test us and where we have to draw on our expertise, professionalism and experience to help care for a child and their family. Families being helped by the Neighbourhood Care Scheme often seem to be in a 'blip' in their lives, and I feel as though I am contributing a lot of my own experience or ideas, in helping that family get through their bad patch.

When the children go to bed at night, and say how cosy and warm the bed is, they talk about what we have done during the day. It makes it all worthwhile, knowing that by including the children in a family environment, the time they are separated from their parents is eased, and they feel as though they have had a special time that day.

Some children never go shopping with their parents, as the parent may be too ill, or the child may come from a big family and the parent may find it easier not to take everyone. As one parent, said 'I can't hold the trolley and run round after my son, so I don't take him'. I involve the children in my weekly shopping trips, starting from the basics of shopping and walking round together, pushing the trolley, picking the items from the shelves and discussing colours, prices, and types of containers. A relaxed learning trip, encouraging the children to investigate healthy, affordable foods. The children can help to prepare and cook the food that has been bought and try it for tea. It is also great when the child can tell their parents about different meals they have tried.

A trip to my local paper shop is a great experience for a child. The local shops know the job which I do and they give the children special attention. I send each child to the counter to pay for their own crisps, reminding them of their 'please' and 'thank-you', and they feel great, and grown up. The assistants will talk to each child and make them feel included, and I will watch from a short distance feeling proud of them.

I have met a lot of people along the way in this job; from little children for whom we are there for all their needs, to going for a burger and finding that the person serving was one of the children I looked after!

My children were just starting school when we started working for the Neighbourhood Care service. They have grown up in the environment of other people's children being in their home. They are all adults now, and have become caring, thoughtful and understanding to other people and their children.

The Neighbourhood Care Service offers a twenty-four hour support telephone line to carers working for them. Each month each carer has a supervision meeting with their support worker to see how all the placements are progressing. We have the opportunity to discuss any problems and successes, whether we need any additional equipment, resources or advice. Some placements can be difficult and challenging with a lot of work and time spent – but all worthwhile when we see a breakthrough and positive results to a difficult situation. Each week the carers have the opportunity to attend a support group session, where carers can meet and talk, and the children can play together, which can be very beneficial. This can be particularly helpful when a large sibling group has been split up and are being looked after by two carers, and these sessions enable those children to have the chance to play together and see each other.

Support Care is my career after so many years. Birmingham's Neighbourhood Care service has a regular training programme and it is a real job. Yes, there can be a lot of sheets to wash, toilet handles to keep mending, and lots of shopping to do – where people think I'm buying for a month although it is just for the week. Many families and children are waiting for a break because of a current crisis in their lives or ongoing difficulties, and Support Care really can help. My experience is that it does work.

Chapter 8

A Stitch in Time

Pat Bugajski

Introduction

This chapter is about the Short Breaks scheme in Stockport and I am writing in my capacity as co-ordinator. The work is presented through a series of case studies, which demonstrate the need for Support Care. The potential and usefulness of Support Care to service users is shown by its preventing children becoming permanently 'looked after' by the local authority where that is not in their best interest. A 'stitch in time' does, in most cases, prevent further extensive intervention.

The Short Breaks scheme went live in April 2002 and, at its height, twelve carers were providing placements for twenty-seven children. There is scope for expansion and there has been considerable expression of interest from potential new Short Break providers.

I arrange Support Care for children who live at home with their families where there is some form of crisis and a need for support whilst the family get their lives back together again. The Short Breaks project aims to provide children and their families with some breathing space: to prevent family breakdown during this critical period; and to avoid the need for the child to be 'accommodated' full-time. My role is to take referrals, match the families to carers, organise meetings and provide support where needed. However, this chapter is not about what I do but about the families and carers who are at the centre of the project and who are the people who really make it a success. I think we should never underestimate the importance of preventing a child being accommodated full-time, when they could remain living at home with the right sort of support.

Case studies

Sam

Sam is a ten-year-old boy living at home with his mother, Janine and his younger brother and sister. He plays with three other children and seems happy and contented. His mother looks on and tells me they have had a lovely summer holiday and that when the children return to school she plans to start a college course and develop her computer skills. Nothing unusual about this you may think. Well, actually there is.

Sam has a diagnosis of Attention Deficit Hyperactivity Disorder (ADHD) and the family experienced a number of difficulties coping with his behaviour and struggled to give the other children any time. Janine's former partner tried to offer support but was unable to understand or manage Sam's behaviour and resorted to over-chastising him. Sam's name was put on the Child Protection register and he was placed in a children's residential unit. Janine felt that, on her own, she would be unable to cope. She was suffering from stress because of everything that had happened and the breakdown of her relationship with her partner.

Sam's placement in the children's residential unit broke down. It was agreed that Sam could return home whilst a full-time foster placement was found. The social worker referred Sam to the Short Breaks project to access support for the family and help reduce the pressure during the summer holiday, whilst a suitable full-time placement was found. Janine was very anxious about how she was going to manage.

The day after I met Janine for the first time, I was invited to a meeting. This was attended by a number of professionals including the head teacher of Sam's school, his social worker and a member of the Children and Adolescent Mental Health Services team. It was a difficult meeting and a number of people aired concerns about how a suitable placement had not yet been found and about Sam living at home. Janine was clearly upset and quite angry. She told everyone she was fed up with hearing these things and that she wanted her son to stay at home and that this is what he also wanted. She knew they were struggling and she really did not know how they were going to manage but she said she wanted to try.

The Short Breaks scheme offered Sam a placement that involved him being looked after by a Short Breaks carer, Alison, in the carer's home, from nine in the morning until four thirty in the afternoon on weekdays during the holiday. Alison also provided daycare for four other children around Sam's age. Alison is a warm, nurturing, organised woman who is passionate about what she does, and does it well.

Sam and his mother received a warm welcome in her home. Alison explained how she sits down with the children to help them plan their activities for the school holiday. This allows the children to do the things they want to do themselves as well as try out new things. She spoke to Sam with respect and understanding and gave him some very clear messages that she would make every effort to ensure that he enjoyed his time with her and have fun. In return, Sam was expected to operate within the boundaries she imposed, to ensure that all the children in her care could be safe, and happy, and get the most out of their time with her. Alison explained what these boundaries were and checked that Sam agreed to this.

There is a firmness about Alison, and you can tell that she does not take any 'messing' and means what she says. Yet at the same time she exudes warmth and caring and what she says makes sense. Janine warmed to her straight away and felt that this was not someone who would take over but someone who was offering them a lifeline and providing exactly the type of help and support they needed to stengthen Sam's placement at home.

The first paragraph of this case study described the scene at Alison's home when we reviewed Sam's placement at the end of the summer holiday. I observed the interactions between Alison and Janine and felt proud of the way they had worked together. They had liaised closely during the holiday and Janine had received many positive messages and much support. Alison has not just taken an interest in Sam alone but had been pleased to hear how Janine had been coping and that she had welcomed the time she had been able to give to her two younger children. She had spoken to Janine about the importance of doing things for herself, and Janine had decided to act on this now that her youngest child was due to start nursery. Janine was no longer an angry and frightened woman who feared that she would struggle to cope from one day to the next. She is now a woman who is positive about their future and has moved on.

Chloe

Chloe is a thirteen-year-old girl living at home with her mother and six brothers and sisters. Chloe is the middle child and does not have any contact with her father. Her behaviour has always been reported as being difficult to manage both at home and at school. Three years ago Chloe was diagnosed as having ADHD for which she received calming medication on a regular basis. Chloe's mother, Sadie, tried her best to cope with the needs of the children but has struggled at times on a number of levels. Sadie is unsupported by the fathers of her children, suffers from bouts of depression and was unemployed for some years because of her health problems and the need to care for seven children.

Sadie had contacted social services herself at times to ask for support when she had felt she could manage no longer. She is a committed parent and has never asked social services to remove any of her children from home, even when the going has been very tough indeed. However, two years ago, Chloe was removed on an emergency basis because it was considered Sadie was unable to control or keep Chloe safe from harm. Sadie had been unable to stop Chloe leaving the family home on several occasions and did not know where she had gone. Chloe was known to approach strangers – at any time of the day or night – asking them for cigarettes and money, regardless of their age or gender.

Chloe was placed with a foster carer for two weeks whilst plans were made to return her home with a support package. This was a distressing experience for the whole family who are very close. Sadie felt let down because she thought she had worked in partnership with social services to the best of her ability and yet her child had been removed without any warning. Chloe hated social services and saw them as the enemy. It is taking time for the family to regain their trust in social workers and perhaps they never totally will.

I remember meeting Sadie and Chloe for the first time when I visited them to discuss what the Short Breaks project could offer them if they wanted our involvement. On that occasion I also met some of Chloe's brothers and sisters, Pete (sixteen), Jake (fifteen), Phoebe (eight) and Elly (seven). I was impressed with the children and how they contributed to the discussion, especially Pete and Jake. I felt great respect for their mother. Despite the fact she had had a really tough time, she had clearly done a good job in parenting her children.

Chloe was placed with Jen and Ian who are Short Break foster carers. Both work full-time but commit every other weekend (and the occasional evening) to providing placements to support children living at home. They are a young couple with a great sense of humour and a wonderful rapport with teenagers. The aims of Chloe's placement were essentially to give Chloe and her mother some breathing space during a particularly difficult period at home whilst support from other services was also offered to address some identified issues and improve the situation in the home. The placement has been successful and there have been many areas that have been improved upon.

From Chloe's point of view, she has spent time with Jen and Ian who have been committed to helping her address some issues that have been pertinent to her. For example, Chloe has had some problems with food and there was a query over whether this was due to the medication she was on for the ADHD or whether it was attention-seeking behaviour. There were concerns about the amount of weight she was losing. From the first time Chloe visited Jen and Ian she had been part of the whole process of planning, buying the ingredients and preparing the meal. This was far from being a lesson in domestic science but a fun activity, which Jen and Chloe enjoy.

Chloe is a bright young woman but her behaviour at school had prevented her from developing her academic abilities. Jen bought games, which were fun to play, but also helped to develop Chloe's literacy and numeracy skills. Chloe also enjoyed being able to roll out of her bed on a Saturday morning to hog the bathroom for an hour. Having a long, uninterrupted foam bath is not a luxury you can experience when sharing a bathroom with six other people. Chloe is an active young woman who enjoys ten-pin bowling and football. Jen and Chloe are ardent Manchester United supporters.

Sadie has enjoyed the time when Chloe has been on Short Breaks because it has allowed her time with her other children whose needs she feels are sometimes ignored because Chloe takes up so much of her time. Sadie has also had an excellent relationship with Jen and Ian; they have worked in partnership sharing news and ideas to address issues when they arise. During the time Short Breaks has been involved there has been a multi-agency approach to address long-standing problems relating to housing, health and education. The family's situation is now stabilised, they have made excellent progress and there is no longer a risk of Chloe needing to be removed from home.

Mark and Joe

Mark (aged ten) and Joe (aged eight) live at home with their mother, Susie. Susie had a very difficult relationship with her ex-husband, which included domestic violence. The family situation is too complex to detail in full but needless to say Susie had a great deal to manage. These difficulties had an adverse effect on her children's behaviour, relationships and their attitude towards women. Susie had experienced numerous problems coping with Mark's behaviour in particular, as he was often verbally and physically aggressive towards her and Joe. At the time I met Susie she was suffering from stress and depression and felt unable to cope.

My intention was to offer both Mark and Joe Short Breaks placements in order that they could all have some breathing space. However, Mark was adamant that he did not want a placement and the project will only place children who are in agreement with the plan. Joe, on the other hand, liked the idea of Support Care and so a placement was set up for him. Joe initially spent one full day a weekend, which was later increased to two days every week after he requested this. Susie also felt it would help the family during a particularly difficult time.

Sally and Jeff have four children of their own (aged between eleven and seventeen) and a five-year-old foster child placed with them full-time. They are a dynamic and flexible couple who are dedicated to offering a service to children experiencing difficulties. They are both committed to working with children in crisis and have an understanding and sympathetic attitude towards children who may display challenging behaviour.

The carers worked in partnership with Susie who sometimes rang them in the evenings when she was having difficulties at home. Sally and Jeff were happy to provide Susie with this support but there were occasions when they felt Susie needed additional help and then, with Susie's knowledge and consent, they contacted social services out-of-hours service.

When Joe first started his Short Breaks placement he had very low self-esteem and little confidence. In the home he spoke in a weak and barely audible voice and tended to curl up on Susie's lap in the foetal position. Sally and Jeff have focused on helping Joe become positive and assertive. They have encouraged Joe to take part in new activities to develop his confidence and boost his self-esteem. Joe was terrified of trying new things but with much patience and encouragement he has gone swimming, learnt to ride a bike and has taken up football, which he thoroughly enjoys. Susie was pleased with his progress and further encouraged this by arranging for Joe to join a local football team.

Joe's placement has been successful on a number of levels and provided him with a sympathetic ear and a safe place when things have been particularly stressful at home. Mark is now undergoing an assessment by a specialist team to find out what support he needs to address his complex difficulties. Although Mark never committed himself to the Short Breaks placement he was offered, he has visited Sally and Jeff and benefited from the support they have given his mother and brother. The carers reduced the high level of tension in the home, which might have led to both children needing to be removed had this support not been around. Although this family still have a long way to go they have the opportunity of facing their problems together.

Mattie

Mattie is eight years of age and lives at home with his mother, Julie. When I first met Julie I was impressed by her clear devotion to her son but concerned about her level of stress. She was twenty-four years of age and did not feel able to contemplate going out socially without Mattie, as there was no one willing to look after him because of his difficult behaviour. There were problems both with his behaviour and his ability to get on with other children and adults. Julie had to manage Mattie's behaviour on her own in the home and felt isolated and unable to see an end to her problems.

Mattie was provided with a day support placement with a Short Breaks carer, Cherry. During term time he went to Cherry's twice a week after school. During the school holidays Mattie went two or three days a week. At first Mattie was worried about going, as he knew there would be other children around and feared he may not get on with them. Julie was nervous about him going and although she thought the idea was good in theory, she didn't think it would work for them in practice.

Mattie settled at Cherry's very quickly and the placement has been a success. Mattie, Julie and Cherry have worked hard to make this placement work which has paid off with them achieving some great results. Julie and Cherry have liaised with each other closely and discussed issues openly and honestly. They have shared information and ideas in order to ensure consistency and stability for Matthew to develop. With Julie's permission, Cherry has also liaised with the school to gain and share information to resolve issues that have arisen during the placement. Mattie established good relationships with Cherry and the other children in her care. Mattie developed socially and no longer operates outside of his group of peers and has become a 'team player'.

Encouraged and supported by Cherry, Julie has been enabled to have time without Mattie. Until her involvement with Short Breaks, Julie has always felt she had sole responsibility for caring for Mattie and that having a social life would simply not be an option until Mattie was much older. However, her thinking is now clearer and she is more confident and her views on this changed. Julie is much happier and is now in a relationship. None of this has been plain sailing but all of it has been worth it. It is lovely to take part in a review meeting and to hear how all their hard work has paid off. There is nothing better than seeing that a family no longer needs a placement because they have moved on, have grown stronger and are able to manage on their own.

Josh

Josh is thirteen years of age and is a big Manchester United supporter. He loves football, music, hanging out with his friends and he occasionally gets on the wrong side of his teachers in school. Although Josh presents as your average teenager, I am aware that his life has been far from average and he has had many problems to cope with for someone so young. Josh has lacked consistency and stability in his life having been received into care on a number of occasions because of his mother's chaotic lifestyle and use of drugs. He moved to live with his grandmother eight years ago and his mother has had no contact with him since. Josh had a close relationship with his grandmother but sadly she died last year.

Josh went to live with his Uncle Steve, and his partner, Val. Val has four children from a previous relationship, aged between seven and sixteen years. Initially they agreed to Josh living with them, thinking that one more teenager wouldn't be a problem. However, they hadn't anticipated how difficult it would be to understand and meet Josh's particular needs. Josh was in need of warmth, love, nurturing and stability. Steve and Val wanted to give him these things and believed the best way to do this was to treat him in exactly the same way as the other children. However, Josh's emotional difficulties made it difficult for him to conform to the same basic house rules as everyone else. As a consequence of this, Josh often found that he had privileges withdrawn and felt unhappy and unloved. Josh was referred to the Short Breaks project at a time when Steve and Val felt unable to cope anymore and requested additional support to avoid the placement breaking down completely.

Josh was placed with Kay and Liam, who live with their son and three foster children. They have been carers for a number of years and whilst they still provide full-time foster placements, they are also involved in providing day support packages of Support Care for the Short Breaks project. Kay is the main carer with Liam actively supporting her role. Kay wants to make a difference and has a reputation for being able to understand and work with children and young people who may have challenging behaviour. She has a sympathetic and honest approach and is able to work well with families who have experienced a variety of problems. Kay has reached the point of being 'unshockable' and is able to take most things in her stride. Her home is often busy and always welcoming.

After consulting with Steve, Val and Josh, it was clear that the type of placement required would need to be flexible to meet the family's needs. Josh was feeling insecure and his original motivation to agree to the placement was to give Steve and Val a break. It was agreed that Josh would spend time with Kay on alternate Sundays to see how he got on and then, if he wanted more contact, he could attend weekly for support. It was also agreed that if things became fraught at home Josh could contact Kay out of office hours and spend extra time with her and her family. On these occasions, Kay would contact Steve or Val to confirm that Josh was with her.

Josh settled into his placement very quickly, enjoyed spending time with another family and developed some very positive relationships. Josh tends not think about the consequences of his actions and has recently got into trouble with the police again for petty offences. Previously this would have put his placement with Val and Steve at risk. They find it very difficult to understand why Josh commits these offences and they worry that this may have a negative impact on the other children in their home. However, during these stressful periods Kay has been available to provide Josh and his family with the support they have needed to get through. This has helped everyone to remain positive and focused on the excellent progress Josh has made and continues to make and he has avoided making the few mistakes he now makes out of context.

At the time of writing, Josh is still involved with the Short Breaks project, and is doing well. He is more settled and secure, living with Steve and Val, who are very committed to him and who no longer make threats to place him in care if he makes a mistake. The pressure is off and Josh is making progress. I believe this placement would have broken down if they had not received support at a critical time.

Hopes for the future

Evidenced by the case studies the Short Breaks project has provided a flexible service to families experiencing difficulties and has offered realistic and acceptable alternatives to full-time placements. The Stockport project is still small and has great potential, but would benefit from additional funding: this would enable an increase in size to allow all families at risk of potential breakdown the opportunity to access this service and thus prevent future costly intervention and deployment of resources. This service is cost effective for agencies and, most importantly, is beneficial as a preventative intervention for children and their families. The service has shown it is a *stitch in time*.

Chapter 9

Maintaining Attachments: Part-Time Fostering as a Preventative Intervention Model

Jacqui Westwood

Introduction

This chapter looks at the provision of Part-time Foster Care to prevent family breakdown and provides a theoretical background to its use. It details the current practice in Telford and Wrekin and uses examples of successful outcomes for children (even though one case study is included where a child cannot remain with their own family) through the preservation of their attachments to their main caregivers. Telford and Wrekin is a unitary authority: there are currently 208 Looked After Children, 111 of whom are placed within 94 in-house foster placements, and the remainder are in external fostering and residential therapeutic environments.

The information contained within the chapter has been gathered as a consequence of an evaluative piece of research examining the success of the Part-time Fostering Scheme by looking at fifty-three part-time placements provided by eight households over the last four years, with the intention of making recommendations for the possible expansion of the scheme. The evaluation took place in March and April 2004, and involved semi-structured interviews with eight part-time foster carers, and evaluative questionnaires disseminated to case management social workers placing the children in their care. This chapter outlines a record of success from Telford and Wrekin in contributing to the reduction in family breakdown and stabilising relative care and long-term foster placements.

The Department of Health (DoH) clearly acknowledges:

Parenting can be challenging. It often means juggling with competing priorities to balance work and home life as well as trying to understand

how best to meet children's needs, at all stages of their development.
Parents themselves require and deserve support. Asking for help should be
seen as a sign of responsibility rather than as a parenting failure.
(DoH, 1999: 1)

This is one of the first paragraphs in this important DoH document and is a
fundamental message to consider when thinking about the services we offer
to children and families in need.

Social work experience leads me to believe that in practice we often
pathologise families, and perceive them as inadequate if they come to the
attention of social services departments. However, the current government
agenda, following the inquiry into the death of Victoria Climbié (Laming,
2003) and the subsequent consultation paper *Every Child Matters* (HM
Treasury, 2003), is leading the way for a shift in focus to that of early
detection and prevention, which is now intrinsic to the Children Act 2004.
The emphasis is now on better identification, working together, and
supporting parents and carers to prevent children being received into care.
The emphasis is also on reducing the number of cases of child abuse and
subsequent child death, which have often shared the theme of lack of early
preventative intervention. The government also has a focus on fostering and
adoption services in terms of ensuring that children remain firmly attached to
their primary carers. This was clearly evident in the government's *Quality*
Protects initiatives which stated that one of the key objectives for local
authorities was to identify ways to support families in the community to
prevent children from entering the care system (DoH, 1998).

Theoretical background

The provision of part-time foster care offered to families in crisis as a
preventative intervention model is clearly underpinned by attachment theory.
We cannot begin to explore the purposes of this provision without addressing
the theory, which provides the foundation for the service. Of the many writers
and researchers who have looked at the relationship between early attachment experience and the effects on all areas of a child's development, one of
the most influential has been Fahlberg. She is clear that:

> . . . *when children have a strong attachment to a parent, it allows them to*
> *develop both trust for others and self-reliance. These earliest relationships*
> *influence both physical and intellectual development as well as forming the*
> *foundation for psychological development.*
(Fahlberg, 1994: 14)

Hughes also reminds us that the majority of children found in the care system
demonstrate behaviours which could be classified as attachment disorganisa-
tion or reactive attachment disorder. Both disorders are thought to arise from

maltreatment by parents, severe physical and emotional neglect and multiple caregivers. 'In both groups the developing child is left with significant deficits in his or her ability and readiness to trust and rely on his or her new caregivers . . .' (Hughes, 2002: 7). He is also clear about the far-reaching and long-lasting effects of inadequate development of attachments. This is a factor when thinking about the reasons why children enter the care system, the effects of their earlier life experiences and the effect of the experience of long-term separation from their main caregiver. Research tells us that primary attachment experiences underpin subsequent relationships and are critical to the psychological, emotional and physical development and well-being of the child.

Early research on attachment was reliant on white Eurocentric perspectives, which described the primary caregiver as the mother. However, recent work has attempted to move from a dyadic way of thinking about exclusive mother-and-baby attachments, to that of attachment networks, where children develop secure attachments with other available caregivers. This move towards thinking about the development of attachments as a continuum is beneficial when planning services such as part-time foster placements. The placements are organised to allow for the development of regular, planned episodes of care with the same foster carer. This allows the child to feel comfortable and confident and in some cases, as the evaluation found, provided an opportunity for the development of attachments to other significant adults. This consistency also minimises the damage caused by multiple moves and allows the parents to feel comfortable about the arrangement. The use of the same carer for each child also means that within the Fostering Service Regulations (DoH, 2002 (Regulation 37)) the placements can be treated as a single placement, which is beneficial to local authorities in terms of their performance indicators.

Alongside attachment theory, theories of child development are also important when attempting to match children's needs and carer's skills in placements. According to the *Framework for the Assessment of Children in Need and their Families*:

> *A thorough understanding of child development is critical to [all] work with children and families. Children have a range of different and complex developmental needs which must be met during different stages of childhood if optimal outcomes are to be achieved . . .*

(DoH, 2000: 10)

Having considered the reasons why protecting the fragile attachments of children to their main caregiver is so vital, we can now consider the formation of a preventative model of family support which is underpinned with this knowledge base.

Development of the Part-time Fostering Scheme

Following research into the outcomes of children leaving care, in terms of educational attainment, employment and general life opportunities, the government initiative *Quality Protects* defined several objectives for social services departments. Two of these were:

> ... *to ensure that children are securely attached to carers capable of providing safe and effective care for the duration of childhood, [and ...] to support families in the community to avoid the necessity of children being received into the Looked After System and experiencing disruption and damage detrimental to their well-being.*

(DoH, 1998)

My post was subsequently funded as a result of this initiative, with a specific remit to design and implement a 'preventative' form of fostering.

In September 1999 I began the research, designed the scheme, designed the review format, undertook the recruitment, and the first carers for the part-time fostering scheme were approved in February 2000. Since then there has been a steady flow of foster carers interested in this scheme, particularly those who work full time, so we have a constant nucleus of around twelve placements. The focus of the placements is to offer short-term, task-focused episodes of foster care to children and young people at the point when a family is in acute crisis and breakdown may be imminent. The placements are not offered in circumstances of identifiable long- term and chronic family dysfunction, where there is a history of on-going failed social services involvement with little prospect of recovery.

The placements are task-centred: identified aims and objectives are established at the outset and reviewed regularly throughout the placement. Task-centred practice is suitable for families experiencing a temporary but acute crisis who are not in a state of chronic, complex crises or long-term dysfunction. The service user has to acknowledge the problem, which can be resolved by actions taken outside of contacts with workers invoking self-determinism on the part of the service user. The problems need to be clearly definable and the service user must want to make the changes necessary to bring about stability in their lives again.

There is some evidence that: children who have experienced part-time placements have not subsequently entered the care system; and long-term placements with foster carers have been maintained following this type of intervention, thereby sustaining children's attachments to their primary carers. The placements are intended to be planned, responsive, to keep families together, maintain children's school and community links, prevent acute problems becoming chronic, empower families to take control, and provide partnership in practice. They result in minimal state intervention and long-term cost effectiveness.

Legal context

During the initial design of the Part-time Fostering Scheme, legal advice was sought regarding modifying or dispensing with the Looked After Children (LAC) paperwork and status. The reason for this was that emerging research, indicates that families were 'put off' using the service if their children became perceived as being 'in care' (Greenfield and Statham, 2004). In addition, families and social workers considered the requirement for medical examination unnecessary. It prevented the opportunity for being flexible and responsive with the service. There were also concerns that if all the children receiving this service were recorded as 'Looked After' then statistics would be skewed regarding numbers of LAC and placement moves. Prior to final recommendations for the scheme, the law and related guidance was explored. The main area of controversy appeared to be in relation to the use of Section 20 or Section 17 of the Children Act 1989 for the provision of the placements.

Children Act 1989 Section 17(1) – refers to children in need, with every local authority having a duty to promote the upbringing of children in need by their families.

Children Act 1989, Part III, Provision of Accommodation, Section 20 (4) – where the local authority may provide accommodation for any child within their area (even though a person who has parental responsibility for them is able to provide accommodation) if they consider that to do so would safeguard or promote the child's welfare.

Currently, Telford and Wrekin use Section 20 (4) of the Children Act 1989, which means the child is 'accommodated' because they are receiving care for 24 hours or more. However, we have modified the amount of Looked After Children paperwork, which, although not a legal requirement, is dictated by 'good practice'. The paperwork used currently is the *Essential Information Record Part I, Placement Plan Part II* and an in-house review document. We have dispensed with the need to request a medical examination unless there are specific medical concerns. This is a compromise position but one which still causes confusion to children's social workers. The evaluation we conducted of the Telford and Wrekin's Part-time Fostering Scheme produced a similar conclusion to that of Greenfield and Statham (2004), in that for this type of service provision clear government guidance is required for consistent practice.

The placements are currently provided and managed by the Fostering Service and they are overseen by fostering social workers. Therefore, we must also consider the appropriate regulations in relation to the Care Standards Act 2000 (DoH, 2002).

Fostering Service Regulations 2002 Regulation 37 – allows for a series of pre-planned placements, with the same carer, to be treated as a single placement so long as the series occurs within one year, has no single placement longer than 4 weeks and the total in the year does not exceed 120 days (DoH, 2002).

National Minimum Standards 2002 Standard 31 – relates to the provision of policies and procedures where the fostering service provides short-term breaks (DoH, 2002).

During the evaluation the legal complexities of the placements were explored. I realised that changes in Ofsted's Regulations (DfES, 2003) permitted child-minders to become registered to provide overnight care for up to 27 days. However, I understand that in Telford and Wrekin, uptake of registration by child-minders to offer this service has been poor.

The Children and Adoption Act 2002 has made the following amendments to the Children Act 1989. Section 116 amends Section 17 subsection (6) (services that may be provided) to include 'providing accommodation'. The Act also makes amendments to Section 22(1) of the Children Act 1989, and excludes children provided with accommodation under Section 17 from being Looked After and having all the LAC policies and procedures applied to them, such as medicals, reviews, etc.

Department of Health guidance states that: Section 17 of the Children Act 1989 includes the power of local authorities to provide accommodation for families and children and that provision of accommodation in this way does not make the child Looked After (DoH, 2003).

Whilst the provision of the placements continues under Section 20(4), the much-needed expansion of the scheme is delayed. However, my recent review of the service is expected to underpin recommendations to senior management regarding the revisiting and amendment of the legal status for placements.

The Part-time Placement Process

- Placement referrals are received from Case Managing Social Workers via the duty officer or Resource Allocation Meeting (RAM – this is an admissions panel for all placements).
- The RAM panel agrees that there is an imminent danger of a family breakdown and the subsequent accommodation of a child into the Looked After System.
- The referral is passed to the Family Placement Team who are assured that a Part-time Placement is the most positive option. This may not be the case

if: the referral was for a very young child, where separation from their birth family has been identified as potentially damaging to their attachment to their primary carer; nor where the referral is for an adolescent, and a question arises as to the likelihood of part-time foster care making a significant difference if there is a possibility of relationship problems, which may have persisted for many years.

- Referrals are looked at by the Family Placement Team allocation meeting for matching considerations. The Fostering Social Worker who manages the identified carer then discusses with the case manager the viability of the Part-time Fostering Scheme preventing an accommodation.
- The Case Managing Social Worker then discusses with the family the option of the scheme. The Fostering Social Worker discusses with the identified carer the possibility of the child coming to stay, initially with non-identifiable information.
- A meeting is then arranged for all appropriate people (carers, case manager, the family, sometimes including the child) and this is chaired by the Fostering Social Worker. If it is not appropriate for the child to attend, then their wishes are to be ascertained by the case manager as soon as possible. If agreement to go ahead is reached, then a planning meeting is arranged or can immediately follow the initial meeting if appropriate. If the child was not present at the meeting, the case manager will give the child information about the foster family with the aid of the carer's family book.
- The parent and young person visit the foster family with the case manager and Fostering Social Worker. The case manager arranges transport for the child and parents. At least two subsequent visits to the carer's home will take place; this can include a short visit to have tea etc.
- A 'Placement Agreement' is then drawn up. The initial planning can be for up to six months with the option to terminate at any stage, dependant on funding allocation. The aims of the placement are written down, for example such things as: details of dates and times for placements; transport arrangements; additional tasks, such as case manager to work with the family to look at resolving conflict, family dynamics or to find alternative sources of support within community. Parents remain in control and can terminate the agreement at any stage.
- Placements are then reviewed every two months (three times in six months). These reviews are informal and use a format designed by myself at the outset of the scheme. The purpose of the meeting is to see how the placement is progressing and if any progress is being made at home as a result of the provision. Future plans are made, remaining focused on the termination date usually at six months maximum.

All foster carers providing part-time placements are recruited, trained and assessed in the same way as other mainstream carers. They are paid pro-rata mainstream allowances, with the option of claiming back activity costs if they are agreed at the beginning of the placement.

It is a well-established fact that foster carers are occasionally lost to competing fostering agencies, not because of the money, but because of the lack of support. It has therefore been imperative to ensure that part-time foster carers feel adequately valued and supported. An out-of-hours support system is also available as many of the carers take placements at the weekend when the offices are closed. However, experience of managing the placements has led me to believe that because the carer and the family tend to have a positive relationship, because the service is not forced upon them, but is a voluntary agreement, it is very rare for any issues to arise. All carers providing this service receive:

- An allocated fostering social worker.
- Regular reviews of placement at two monthly intervals.
- Annual foster home reviews.
- Access to the Telford and Wrekin Foster Care Association (run by carers for carers).
- Membership of the Fostering Network.
- The opportunity to access on-going training and undertake an NVQ.
- The option to progress to a carer's fee after 12 months service. This provides a 'reward' or 'payment' element to the carers on top of the maintenance allowance for the child's care.
- Out of hours emergency advice and support.
- Supervisory visits at least once a month, and always within one week of the child's first stay.
- The opportunity to access play therapy, psychological therapeutic services, educational support, holiday and after school activities for all Looked After Children, as appropriate.

Statistics and case examples of Part-time Foster Placements

In order to evaluate the Part-time Foster Scheme, fifty-three placements were identified with eight fostering households. The carers were all interviewed using semi-structured interviews and feedback from the children's social workers was also sought. The results were analysed and collated.

The Telford and Wrekin Part-time Fostering Service is one of few services which have continued to prosper. Of the fifty-three placements examined, sixty-one percent of the children were not subsequently accommodated after receiving a part-time placement; thirty percent remained in their long-term placements after stabilising them, with the use of part-time foster care. These figures show that in ninety-one percent of the fifty-three placements

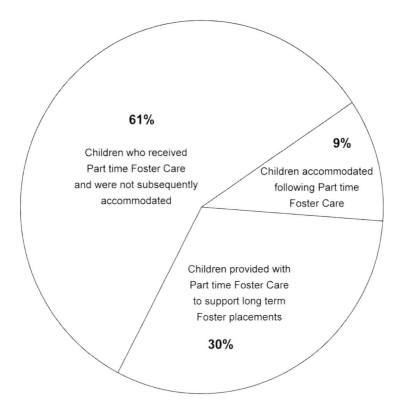

Figure 9.1 Percentage of children who received Part-time Foster Care

considered, children went on to remain living with their primary carers and as a result their attachments were not disrupted.

The following case studies are where part-time foster care was successfully used as a preventative intervention. All identifiable details have been removed from each.

Case studies

Helen and Jessica

Jessica was referred to the family placement team for the provision of a part-time foster placement. She was the daughter of Helen and was just twelve months old. She was of dual heritage and very slight build. Helen was a twenty-one-year-old white woman who lived alone with her daughter. After recently suffering with depression she had threatened to harm her daughter, because she felt she could not cope. Jessica's father, a Black African Caribbean man, had not had any contact with Jessica. Helen had no family support due to their alleged 'racist' views of Helen's relationship with Jessica's father.

On meeting Jessica and her mum, observation of Jessica gave rise to some concerns about her level of attachment to her mother; she presented as indiscriminately affectionate when introduced to the foster carers, whom she had never met before. There were concerns about Jessica having had multiple carers from an early age and the impact this might have had on her attachment to her mother.

Following the introduction to the foster carers and Helen's consent to progress with part-time foster care, a planning meeting was arranged. A number of individual tasks were agreed with Helen, which included looking at part-time college courses, trying to establish friendships locally, making contact with Home Start and looking at her relationship with her own mother to decide if there were any positive elements to it.

Jessica had an initial visit to the carers with Helen, a visit for a few hours alone, and then had her first episode of part-time foster care. This was one whole day a weekend. A review meeting was arranged to ensure the placement was going well, with a child who was so young. The weekend daycare provision continued. At the second review meeting, after four provisions of daycare, it was felt that Helen's progress had been excellent. Helen had now: bought a car; developed some friendships; and enrolled in three part-time college courses for mornings only, which also provided a crèche for Jessica. She had also engaged the services of Home Start, which enabled her to meet other single young mums. She decided to sever her relationship with her mother, feeling that it was one of too much conflict because of Jessica's heritage.

The review decided that Helen had satisfactorily completed the tasks identified and had made excellent progress. She stated that she felt much better and more confident to parent Jessica without the support from social services. The meeting felt confident to discharge the resource and that Jessica was no longer at risk. Jessica and her mum have not come to the attention of Social Services since.

Martin

Martin, an eight-year-old boy, was referred for a part-time placement because his mother was stating that she could no longer cope with him. After further exploration with Martin's social worker, it transpired that Martin had in the past been seriously ill, resulting in him spending large amounts of time in hospital with his mother by his side constantly. She was a single mother and had two other children, one of whom had some special needs in the form of a learning disability. A meeting was organised and Martin's mum was very clearly saying that Martin would not leave her side, was 'suffocating' her and that she was not able to devote any time to her other children. It was agreed that the provision of part-time foster care would allow her to spend more time with her other children, particularly taking her daughter shopping, which she had specifically requested. It was also felt that if Martin could build up a relationship with his carers then he would also learn that he could feel safe with someone else whilst remaining firmly attached to his mum.

Gentle introductions, with Martin's mum's support, were arranged. The identified carers had no other children at home and it was considered that individual attention would be better for Martin, than if he had had to compete with other children. In his placement Martin received a whole weekend once a month. Initially Martin found the placement difficult, and on occasions would cry to go home. However, his carers were supportive and his mum also supported the placement by reassuring Martin that she was not going to leave him. The placement was reviewed regularly as planned and because of the competing needs in Martin's family continued for eighteen months. Whilst not within the original remit of the scheme, as placements normally would only be offered for six months, it was considered that there was a clear need to be flexible in this case and there was not a risk of placement drift as it was carefully monitored.

Over time it was evident that Martin had become very settled and made clear attachments to his carers, who stated that he felt like 'one of the family.' Martin had also become very good friends with the foster carer's young dog, as the two of them had boundless energy!

A final review meeting decided that Martin's mum was now happy with her relationships with all of her children. She herself had entered into a relationship with a man and the children had begun to accept him as part of their life. Martin was much calmer and less demanding of his mum's time and had realised that he was safe to move from mum's side and make new relationships. It was agreed that the placements should be withdrawn with a view to providing some support, via telephone, if needed for a while. Martin had a final visit and appeared ready to move on and leave his part-time foster placement behind. The family have not had any Social Services involvement since.

David

David was ten and had a long history of Social Services involvement. It was felt that because David was in a long-term placement with his grandparents, who were approved as Relative Foster Carers, and because his placement had become very unstable, the offer of some part-time foster care would serve several purposes. The part-time carers would provide an assessment of David's behaviour, as there had been concerns regarding his grandparents' management and the possibility of the use of smacking as a punishment, which is prohibited for all Telford and Wrekin foster carers. The placement would provide David with some time out and a different quality of family life. It would also provide his grandparents with the opportunity to spend time alone together. David was a child who had suffered many traumatic life experiences and grave physical abuse whilst in his mother's care. He had also suffered interfamilial sexual abuse. His behaviour was overactive and demanding, both at home and at school.

A placement was set up where David would be the only child. David was initially quite concerned, fearing he was being 'taken away' from his grandparents. With the carers and his grandparents supporting each other, David soon realised this was not the case. He received one weekend a month, and also had telephone contact to his grandparents whilst in placement, and to his part-time carers when at home.

His part-time placement went well and he enjoyed the attention he received. However, unfortunately there was no evident change at home, despite social work input in the provision of other management strategies. It became evident that his grandparents were not able to manage David and his placement eventually broke down following a Section 47 (Children Act 1989) investigation into him being struck by his grandmother. David was moved to another placement. This subsequently became long-term and for a period David still continued to go to his part-time placement to support his new placement and provide him with consistency. A final review meeting decided that David was very settled. Observations of changes in his behaviour made it apparent that he was evidently happier. It was felt that he no longer needed the provision.

Stephanie and Stuart

Stephanie and Stuart were referred for part-time foster care to help prevent family breakdown. Their parents' relationship was fragile, and their mother was exhausted. The two children were both very demanding and were diagnosed with Attention Deficit Hyperactive Disorder (ADHD). Both children were in constant trouble at school and there were concerns about the level of supervision at home. Stephanie was twelve and her brother, Stuart, was thirteen. Both children were on medication. The purpose of the placement was to allow their parents some time to work on their own relationship and to allow the children some alternative family time. After information exchanges with the family and the identified carers, the two families were introduced and the placement set up.

The children received part-time foster care one weekend a month for ten months. Again, this was longer that the usual six months, but the placement was carefully managed and was necessary to achieve the objectives within the family home.

The carer's assessment of the children agreed that they were very overactive and extremely demanding even with medication. They arranged ongoing activities, which included cycling, swimming and walking in an attempt to keep the children busy and engage them in activities, which reduced their tendency to fight and wind each other up.

During this time their parents were able to spend time together. They went out for meals and even went away for the weekend, twice, in the knowledge that the children were safe and happy. The foster carers spoke to the children's mum and dad regularly and provided telephone support in terms of ideas to manage the children's behaviour between placements. The final review took place after ten months at which time there had been improvements in the parents' relationship and in their ability to parent the children in a united way. The children had even shown signs of improvement at school. It was felt by all that the parents would like to try to manage without the placement but could still receive telephone support for a while, if needed. What transpired was that they didn't even need this, but the offer had reassured them. The Department have had no further involvement with the children.

Conclusion

Having evaluated fifty-three placements and considered the case studies above, it is evident that the common theme emerging is the success in maintaining the precious attachments of the children to their main caregivers. One of the above case studies involved a child who did have to be accommodated by the local authority (David). Here, the Support Care provision offered continuity whilst he settled into his alternative permanent family placement. This case was included to offer a balanced picture of the reality of Support Care and work with children and families; in some cases, despite preventative intervention, some children may still have to be accommodated.

Such preventative intervention, like Support Care, which keeps children's affectionate bonds to significant adults intact, is vital. While preventative intervention, such as Support Care, exists, there can be no justification for damaging such attachments by removing children from their main caregivers, into local authority accommodation.

Part-time foster carers play an important role in meeting children's needs but also in supporting their families, and as a consequence, can help maintain critical attachments to primary carers. The notion of supporting families by the use of part-time foster care placements is not a new one. There is a wealth of evidence that this service is successful in contributing to the sustenance of families and in reducing the disruption of attachments resulting from the receipt of children into care.

Aldgate and Bradley identified the ethos of the Children Act 1989 as being essentially one of 'breaking down the barriers between community-based support and out-of-home placements' (Aldgate and Bradley, 1999: 210). They concluded that part-time or supportive fostering was a service which worked because it was positive, voluntary and community-based and was therefore welcomed by families. Children did not perceive it as 'going into care' and the parents who had accessed the service felt that the carers were 'people like us, but without the problems' (Aldgate and Bradley, 1999: 205).

In our research evaluation, the service was also perceived as inclusive, and social work input that was concurrent with the part-time foster care provision as helpful. The evaluation for Telford and Wrekin found, equally, that the carers interviewed were very satisfied with the service they had been able to offer, and felt that they had played a huge part in preventing family breakdown. One carer said:

One of my placements was a dual heritage sixteen-month-old baby. Mum was in hospital having suffered severe domestic violence at the hands of her husband. The language and cultural issues were a challenge but I know that by supporting that mum whilst she re-established her life without her husband contributed to that mother and baby staying together.

Part-time fostering is attractive to families who work full time and could not otherwise engage in fostering, but would like to. It is also a useful way for carers to 'try out fostering' before making a full-time commitment and equally useful for those wishing to reduce their commitment. Another of our carers, when interviewed said:

We wanted to try fostering and were not sure if we would be able to do it, this way we were able to have a go and now we have a full-time as well as part-time placement. It was good for our children to be introduced gradually.

Of the eight foster families interviewed, only two female carers did not work outside the home, but both were registered childminders.

However, it is necessary to note that whilst there is evidence that children who have been supported through part-time fostering do not usually go on to enter the care system on a full-time basis, it is hard to argue whether or not this is coincidental. These children may not have entered the care system anyway. That being said the general feeling from the carers and the social workers involved during the research evaluation, was that the service was clearly a preventative one and both groups were very positive about its beneficial impact.

As with all pilot schemes, development and redevelopment is endemic. Having undertaken this research into the success of the service, it is apparent that:

- Whilst there remains a clear lack of consistent guidance related to the legal status of the placements this has a bearing on the expansion and speed of access to the service.
- There needs to be clear ongoing monitoring and evaluation to provide quantifiable evidence that there is a consequent reduction in the number of children who become Looked After following the preventive work of this scheme.
- There is a need for further discussion regarding the location of the scheme, and whether it should be in the Family Placement section of the Department or whether, as with other models, it should be ring-fenced as a separate entity.
- There is also possible scope for the exploration, with other community-based preventative services such as Sure Start, of a partnership service.
- The scheme needs to be managed appropriately for the purpose of the National Minimum Standards and Regulations of Fostering Service. There needs to be the commissioning of further research to include the voices of the children and families receiving the service.

It is clear that there is a need to invest in services of this nature to enable parents to continue in their role and prevent children experiencing the damage and disruption received once they enter the care system. Children's primary attachments to their main caregivers are as crucial to them as the food that they eat, in terms of enabling healthy growth of mind and body. Any form of preventative intervention, which allows children to remain within these significant relationships, cannot be underestimated or overstated. There is no substitute for the formation of attachments, and the long-term effects of their disruption are devastating and far-reaching. However, the fragile distribution of limited resources remains a barrier to proactive service expansion.

Webb and Aldgate write that:

. . . respite care will be an important part of the services designed to promote the welfare of children in need, enhance parental responsibility and prevent family breakdown. The next step is to translate the philosophy into reality . . .

(1999: 126)

Although this chapter's content is not strictly 'respite care' but rather is about supportive part-time foster care, I feel that this quote is applicable because there is sufficient evidence from our evaluative research to suggest that this type of fostering does have a place in preventative social work. There is evidence that the provision of supportive care, at the right time, when a family is in acute crisis, can prevent long-term deterioration in families, and disruption of one of the most crucial bedrocks in healthy child development, which is the formation of meaningful attachment relationships to primary carers. This is the foundation for all subsequent relationships throughout the child's life and into adulthood and is the one thing that can have the biggest and most damaging impact if not preserved.

References

Aldgate, J. and Bradley, M. (1999) *Supporting Families Through Short Term Fostering*. London: The Stationery Office.

DfES (2003) *Day Care and Child Minding (National Standards) (England) Regulations*. London: The Stationery Office.

DoH (1998) *The Quality Protects Programme: Transforming Children's Services*. LAC: 98, 28. London: DoH.

DoH (1999) *Working Together to Safeguard Children*. London: HMSO.

DoH (2000) *Framework for the Assessment of Children in Need and their Families*. London: The Stationery Office.

DoH (2002) *Fostering Services: National Minimum Standards, Fostering Services Regulations*. London: The Stationery Office.

DoH (2003) *LAC 13: Guidance on Accommodating Children in Need and their Families*. London: DoH.

Fahlberg, V. (1994) *A Child's Journey through Placement*. London: BAAF.

Greenfields, M. and Statham, J. (2004) *Support Foster Care: Developing a Short-break Service for Children in Need. Understanding Children's Social Care Series No. 8*. London: Institute of Education.

HM Treasury (2003) *Every Child Matters*. London: The Stationery Office.

Hughes, D. (2002) Forward, in Archer, C. and Burnell, A. (2003) *Trauma, Attachment and Family Permanence. Fear Can Stop You Loving*. London: Jessica Kingsley.

Laming, H. (2003) *The Victoria Climbié Inquiry: Report of an Inquiry by Lord Laming*. London: The Stationery Office.

Webb, S. and Aldgate, J. (1999) Using Respite Care to Prevent Long-term Family Breakdown, in Hill, M. *Signposts in Fostering. Policy, Practice and Research Issues*. London: BAAF.

Chapter 10

A Positive Response

Isabelle Boddy and Jon Plant

Introduction

The Short Break scheme in Hull has been in existence since 1998, when there was a radical shift in how services were offered to children and families. Since then various aspects of the scheme have changed; location, composition, and also to some degree its objectives, but its primary focus still remains the same – to support children to remain at home with their families. This chapter will trace the setting up of the scheme and highlight the initial difficulties encountered; it will then look at how the scheme has developed over the years to meet the ever-changing demands of the dynamic world of social care. It will also look at the strengths of working with children and families in this way and explore the organisational difficulties inherent in an environment competing for resources.

Children in need in Kingston upon Hull

The deprivation in the city of Kingston upon Hull has been long acknowledged, born out of a history of low employment and little in the way of natural resources. Its life originally came from the sea, not from trade with the Americas or Africa, but with the Baltics and from fishing in the treacherous North Sea. The social problems Hull encounters today are much the same as any large city, but somewhat exacerbated by its isolation and lack of employment now the fishing industry is all but extinct. It was against this backdrop that Kingston upon Hull Social Services set up a Children in Need Project in 1995. There is not space here to discuss the project in detail but reference will be made to particular aspects. However, one of the areas looked at was matching needs and services within social services, the purpose of which was to assist in the re-focusing of children's services in line with the requirements of the Children Act 1989. As part of an audit carried out at the time the views of service users were elicited, and the findings helped shape the re-organisation of services in Kingston upon Hull, resulting in a shift towards preventative family support services.

As a result, in 1998, two Family Support Teams were set up, one in West Hull and one in East Hull. They were multi-agency resources and were operated and staffed differently from the traditional childcare social work teams. They offered a range of support services to children and families; packages were put together based on assessment of individual need. The Short Breaks teams were based in the family centres and were thus seen to be firmly in the family support arena.

Short breaks – care or family support?

Short breaks are a special form of care that can be provided by local authorities under Section 20 of the Children Act 1989 to support families who are experiencing difficulties. As such they are subject to particular restrictions, i.e. the placements cannot last longer than twenty-eight days, they must be with the same carer and must not exceed an annual total of ninety days. Many schemes have been set up to assist families with children with a disability, but they also have a huge part to play in a wider family support role.

In a family support context, short breaks can be planned and focused, they can be task-centred, and carers can work on difficulties with families to ensure a continuity of approach. Carers can offer advice and support to families at a time when social workers are not available. Children can benefit from a period of respite, away from a stressful home environment, with the knowledge they will be returning to their families. Short Breaks schemes therefore fitted the ethos of the refocusing on prevention in Kingston upon Hull.

It also means that carers can have full-time jobs or family commitments and are still able to offer occasional breaks for children, and carers who are available during the day can offer daycare or overnight placements to suit a particular need.

Clearly the first consideration when setting up a short-break fostering scheme is, where to base it? It may appear initially more sensible to place it in the already established fostering team or department; after all they will have the trained staff expertise and systems, and they have funding. However, in Kingston upon Hull it was decided that the scheme should be placed firmly in the Family Centres. It was then seen as a positive option for families and not one of last resort. The decision to keep the scheme distinct from the mainstream has been the best decision for the overall success of the scheme, but has brought with it some tension and difficulties. Some of this has been resolved over the years, but some remains, and may, I suspect, always do so.

In the beginning – pitfalls and problems

Recruitment and training

Recruitment of suitable foster carers is a nationally acknowledged difficulty and Hull is no exception. There were anxieties from the fostering department that recruitment for short break carers would inevitably detract from the recruitment of mainstream carers.

Although carers who wish to offer short breaks are often only able to offer a few days a month, they are still subject to the same training and lengthy assessment processes. It was some time therefore, before the family centres had any carers who were attached to the scheme. The placements could only be provided as part of a package of support to ensure other work was being done to address any difficulties and they were only offered to maintain children with their families. This could include kinship carers or adoptive families but not mainstream carers.

There were problems in having an east and west divide in the city; Kingston upon Hull really is a city of two halves! East and West Hull are very different in geography and attitude and perceive themselves to be very different from each other. This became more apparent in the subsequent development of the family centres and the services their users wanted. Initially however, the difficulties were around communication and continuity of practice as well as inconsistency in resources.

The Short Break scheme was staffed by only one family placement officer in each centre who was responsible initially for everything, from recruitment and support to setting up systems for referral and placement. There was a heavy reliance on the fostering team for advertising and recruitment and training. One of the family placement officers was experienced but the other was not, and this caused problems when training and assessing carers. There were also the inevitable difficulties in communication when people who are doing the same job are based in different locations.

In addition, if there were limited places on a 'Choosing to Foster' course then, understandably, they were given to mainstream carers rather than people who only wanted to foster a few days a month. One or two mainstream carers moved to the new scheme but there was no overall drive to do this and there has been no drift, in this direction, across the years.

As previously stated, recruitment of suitable carers is always difficult and there is huge difficulty in recruiting carers who will look after teenagers and boys over eight years old. Most referrals are for these children. There is an abundance of carers willing to take babies or toddlers, and whilst there *is* a demand for these, the greatest area of need is for the older children, especially boys.

Payments and reviews

Like other short-break and respite care schemes Kingston upon Hull had the same difficulties with statutory Looked After Children (LAC) reviews that other authorities had experienced. Now, the first LAC review is held after the child has been going into the placement for occasional days for three months. However, they are not subject to health plans or Personal Education Plans, since the family retains full parental responsibility for the child, and any health or educational issues are addressed by the family with the support of their social worker.

Payment for short-break carers was also another contentious area. Since the periods of care they offer are flexible and often vary, they are paid in blocks of time. They are paid a higher hourly rate than mainstream carers and it is emphasised to them that the money is to provide a positive experience for the child as well as cover costs for food and other expenses. If they have a child in placement for a week the payment they receive is higher than that of mainstream carers and this has caused some friction between departments and carers.

Resolutions – perhaps!

Time, even for families in distress, moves on, and things change. The family support centres continued to evolve, and initial difficulties with the inception of the Short Break scheme were, to some extent, resolved. The issues concerning the family placement officers resolved themselves as the individual workers grew in experience and were able to fully participate in the training and assessment arena. As the scheme grew, another family placement officer was appointed, and they were all based together in one family centre but worked across the whole city.

The issues of competition with mainstream fostering have also eased over the years, and relationships have improved between the two teams. People who offer to participate in the Short Break scheme invariably have commitments that would not permit them to foster on a full-time basis, or, are very clear in their desire to help families look after their children rather than be a substitute family.

Having the scheme based outside the fostering team has caused some issues for senior management, especially with the inception of the Commission for Social Care Inspection (CSCI) and the regular inspection of the fostering service, in terms of registration and accountability, which need careful consideration to resolve here in Hull. These problems are not insurmountable however.

There are clear benefits to the scheme being based in family support. It means resources can be more tightly managed, and although the scheme has always taken children who should have been placed in mainstream resources, the fact that they have different management arrangements ensures some 'gatekeeping'. Because the team is small it means there is greater flexibility in putting together creative packages of support, and each family placement officer knows all of the foster carers and their strengths and weaknesses. This ensures continuity when staff are on leave or otherwise not available.

The Short Break scheme grew in size, but demand has always outstripped supply and this is still the case. The scheme still suffers the same difficulties as mainstream fostering in recruiting and retaining carers for boys of eight years old and upward, and for teenagers. Perhaps we, as a society, need to take a closer look at the way we perceive boy children and how we socialise them.

The following table shows the demand for placements in relation to both gender and age.

Table 10.1 Age at time of referral of all children who had a placement at short breaks between 01/11/03 and 31/10/04

Age group	Male	Female	Total
0–1	11	6	17
2–5	21	12	33
6–9	16	20	36
10–13	23	14	37
14 +	4	18	22
Total	75	70	145

The next stage – or how we learnt to stop worrying and love reorganisation

Life in social work never remains static and re-organisation becomes almost a fact of life, and the subsequent reorganisation of social services in Kingston upon Hull has had a considerable impact on the development of the Short Break scheme.

In 2002, Kingston upon Hull City Council was subject to sweeping reorganisation and there was concomitant restructuring in the social services department. The childcare areas were reorganised into larger teams in line with council areas teams. More crucially, family support teams and childcare social work teams were merged and a new project 'The Out of Hours Team' was set up. This was a huge change for everyone, and as is usually the case, it took a while for the upheaval to settle. The Short Break team was attached to the Out of Hours team and this has led to a change in the way things happen, and an expansion, but not a radical shift in the original remit and ethos of the team.

The Out of Hours team is a new project and consists of an Emergency Duty Team (EDT), a children's home and the Short Break team. The primary function is to offer an out-of-hours family support service to children and families, and to prevent the need for children to be accommodated by outreach work from the residential staff and the EDT. Where children need to be accommodated in the children's home, residential staff start the rehabilitation process immediately and short breaks are offered as part of a longer-term package of support to enable the child to return home as soon as possible. In addition, children may be accommodated in an emergency with a short-break carer and then offered respite or shared care as part of a rehabilitation package.

The changes for the scheme appear small but their impact has been great. When the scheme was placed in the family centres the referrals only came from family support workers and were for planned placements; they were very much part of a support package. However, with the change of location came a change of focus, and requests for emergency placements or respite care at short notice have increased drastically. The referrals now come directly from the area teams or from the EDT. This has meant that some foster carers have had increased numbers of children in placement and a greater turnover of placements. They have had to become more flexible and adept at welcoming children without introductions. Not all the scheme's carers will accept emergencies: they have work commitments, or, do not wish fostering to intrude into their lives too much, which is, for the most part why they became short-break carers. However the carers who do respond are a tremendous bunch and are extremely responsive. It has given their task a different dimension and I am always impressed by their clear child-centred focus; they ensure the child always has a positive experience, despite the distress of the placement being made. Some carers, after having children in placement, have expressed commitment to them and have been approved as specific carers for them as well as maintaining a short-break placement for another child.

The downside

Every attempt is made out of hours to place a child with short-break carers instead of in the childrens' home, especially with very young children. This often means that there is a delay in identifying support that would enable the child to return home. EDT refers these children directly to the area teams, and there is frequently a delay in social workers being allocated and responding, given the work pressure in the teams. This, coupled with the continual lack of mainstream resources, means that often children do get stuck in placements longer than they should, and move-on placements are not as well planned as they should be. There is a great deal of tension between mainstream resources and the scheme when children cannot be moved to long-term placements. This is a common source of difficulty in most schemes, and is the reason, I believe, why family support fostering schemes are better placed outside of traditional fostering departments.

Being part of a new remit has meant an increase in workload for the family placement officers: they now deal with rising numbers of referrals, and we have had to implement a part-time duty system to deal with this. Clearly the more children in placement, the more planning meetings and LAC reviews there are. Family Placement Officers also have ongoing Form F assessments to make (BAAF, 1991) and carers as well as training and support groups to supervise. Recruitment to the scheme has been successful and there are now thirty-one carers with four assessments in the pipeline. This is almost double the number in place when the scheme moved to 'out of hours', and workers are very close to their workload capacity.

The benefits

The benefits for families of access to a planned short break, despite the pressures, are considerable. Primarily, the placement is voluntary and planned with the child and family to meet their needs, no child is ever made to go, being told they have a choice. This often means however, that truculent teenagers will refuse to go, preferring to be near their friends or feeling they are too old to be looked after somewhere else. Yet these are frequently the very families that need support given the difficulties of caring for teenagers in an ever-troubling society. Some carers however are able to build excellent relationships with teenagers (a much prized skill) and can communicate with both sides to help them through difficult times.

The relationships that carers can establish with children's families are crucial to the success of the placement and the overall scheme. They are viewed more as friends than representatives of the local authority, in a way that social workers can never be. They can offer advice about childcare that is accepted because they have experienced looking after the child and know what the problems are; they can consult with the child's carer who, at the end of the day is the expert on the child; they are seen to offer practical help when the family needs it; and there is peace of mind knowing the child is going to a familiar place to be looked after by someone they know.

The scheme has been particularly positive for children whose mothers have mental health difficulties. The children have regular breaks with an identified carer and if their mother becomes very ill or is admitted to hospital they could have a longer break with the carers. The scheme has recently begun to ask all children for their views on their visits to the carers, and comments from children in the above situation are very positive: they feel they can express their worries about their mum to the foster carer, and feel safe. In addition, children in households where the main carer experiences mental health problems often become the carers: regular short breaks give them a positive experience, allowing them to be children again.

One unexpected but positive aspect of the scheme is the recruitment of carers through word of mouth, and the scheme has several mother-and-daughter and best-friend combinations. This allows big groups of siblings to be placed within contact of each other and they can join in family occasions or outings with their brothers and sisters. There is also a bonus for the foster carers who can arrange mutual babysitting arrangements if needed.

Ongoing development – forever onwards

We have attempted recently to use carers more creatively as sessional workers and 'buddies'. For various reasons, including over-anxious and rigid bureaucracy, most of these have not been successful; however, we do have one carer who has trained as a family group conference convenor attached to the scheme, so we are hoping to learn from our mistakes and restart the process. A plan to have dedicated emergency carers attached to the EDT has similarly not been very successful, largely because the carers' usually have other commitments.

The future is bright however. Recruitment to the scheme is fairly lively at the moment and the enthusiasm of the staff and carers is still apparent. There have always been high numbers of children looked after in Hull, although it is not appropriate to delve into the reasons for this here. At the time of the Children in Need Project there were over eight hundred children in local authority care; this has since been reduced to just over six hundred. Clearly many forces were at work to bring down these figures, but the establishing of a flexible system of Support Care must play a powerful part in this reduction. At the present time the Short Break scheme in Kingston upon Hull is supporting over ninety children to remain at home with their families, as well as providing short-term emergency placements. It is however, difficult to estimate how many of these children would have otherwise ended up in the mainstream system.

Short breaks have been used as part of rehabilitation packages for children returning home from long term and emergency care; the placing of the scheme within the 'out of hours' team ensures strong links between the children's home and the outreach services they provide.

The scheme will continue to remain in the family support arm of departmental resources, and, hopefully play a continuing role in reducing the numbers of looked after children by supporting families to care for them, and where possible, enable them to return home speedily when they have been accommodated. The service will continue to strive to work creatively with children and their families to offer a positive alternative to long-term care.

The strategic overview – a senior management perspective

This service was developed in Hull as part of the departmental family strategy, embarked upon in 1997. The context to the strategy was two-fold. Firstly, a growing body of research, most notably highlighted in *Messages from Research* (DoH, 1995), had been backed up by a local research exercise which proved that Hull was indeed a case in point in respect of the need for 'refocusing'. Secondly, a Social Services Inspectorate inspection that had severely criticised children's services reinforced what we already knew – i.e. that Hull's response to children in need was fairly minimal. The response to child protection concerns was often reactive, resulting in high-tariff interventions that were informed by a rigid resource structure which resulted in a disproportionately high number of looked after children.

It was clear that for some families with the greatest needs, accommodation (amongst a range of other interventions) would not only continue to be desirable, but at least for the short term was probably necessary to maintain children's welfare and safety at a 'good enough' level. The trick was to avoid these situations tipping over into a long-term 'looked after' arrangement, whether by default or design, bearing in mind that however optimistically 'looked after' arrangements might be viewed as supporting a plan to return home, the effect was invariably to undermine what was left of the adults' self-confidence as parents, and to further erode family autonomy.

The decision to implement a Short Break service represented a shift in the structural and functional deployment of resources and, just as crucially, a shift in culture and approach. Developed as part of a wider investment in family support provision, the service was part of a recruitment, staff and service development process which aimed to place family support and a strong values-based approach to practice at the heart of all our interventions. Short breaks were therefore to be presented as offering a positive opportunity, rather than the orthodox perception of accommodation as a second-best option, or a last resort. Additionally, the service was to be offered on the basis of a needs assessment (DoH, 2000) and as part of a package of family support, alongside and not in isolation from other interventions. These are the factors that seem to have made the service most amenable to children and families and have underpinned the success of the Short Breaks scheme.

It is worth noting that although the service remains small in comparison to mainstream fostering, in recruitment terms people with a general interest in fostering seem to have been attracted to a more flexible, partnership approach to caring for other people's children. The service has drawn from a population who are motivated less by the idea of providing a more traditional 'substitute family' arrangement, but more by seeing a reward in keeping families together and children out of the care system.

The Short Breaks service is a highly valued part of our family strategy in Hull, and will be increasing in size and scope over the coming years.

References

BAAF (1991) *Form F: Information on Prospective Substitute Parent(s)*. London: BAAF.

Department of Health (1995) *Child Protection: Messages from Research*. London: HMSO.

Chapter 11

Investing to Save?

June Statham and Margaret Greenfields

We need to increase our focus on supporting families and carers – the most critical influence on children's lives. The Government intends to put supporting parents and carers at the heart of its approach to improving children's lives.

(HM Treasury, 2003: 8)

Family support and government policy

The quotation above, from the government green paper *Every Child Matters*, indicated the extent to which family support has become a central aspect of New Labour policy. Since the Children Act 1989 was implemented in 1991, local authorities have had a general duty to promote the care and upbringing of children 'in need'. Under Section 17 of the Act, they are expected to provide services to help such children remain within their families and to avoid the need for them to become 'accommodated' or 'looked after' (these terms were introduced by the Children Act 1989 to replace 'in care', reflecting the fact that out-of-home care should be provided wherever possible with the agreement of parents). The Children Act was not accompanied by significant additional funds, however, and many local authorities struggled to develop preventive family support services as most of their efforts and resources were focused on children who were seen to be at risk of significant harm (DoH, 1995).

Since the late 1990s, there has been an unprecedented amount of government interest in developing better and more widespread services to support children and their families. Alongside policies to support families through taxation and benefits, there has been a wide range of community-based initiatives targeted at disadvantaged areas such as neighbourhood nurseries and Sure Start local programmes for young children and their families, and the Children's Fund to provide support services for children aged five to thirteen. Some key principles underlying the current government's policy on supporting parents are set out in an overview of messages from a major programme of research in this area (Quinton, 2004). They include:

- 'Joined-up' thinking in services at national and local level.
- Partnership with parents in providing services to meet family needs.
- Listening to children's views and needs of services.
- An emphasis on parents' responsibilities as well as their entitlements to support.
- Enabling individuals and families to make the most of their potential, but supporting those in difficulties.
- The importance of good assessments of needs and a good evidence base for planning care and developing services.

Regular short breaks with another family, for children and young people whose own family is struggling to cope, would seem to offer a good example of this kind of support. Such breaks are specifically mentioned in a government review of fostering and placement services called *Choice Protects*, which was launched in 2002 to improve and extend the range of options that local authorities can offer to support children outside of their families. As well as short-term and long-term foster care, 'kinship' care by family and friends, and new types of therapeutic foster care, the *Choice Protects* review refers to a service it describes as 'Support Foster Care'. This combines regular short breaks for children with support for parents, who remain the main carer for their child (DoH, 2002).

There is a history of short-break schemes being set up by local authorities or voluntary organisations for families with a disabled child. These are commonly known as 'family link' or 'shared care' schemes. The evidence suggests that these schemes are much appreciated by parents, although provision is by no means sufficient to meet demand (Tarleton, 2002; Audit Commission, 2003). Official statistics (DoH, 2003), show that some 12,000 children a year are provided with 'an agreed series of short-term placements', although these figures need to be treated with some caution. Local authorities differ in the way they record these series of short-term placements, and the distinction between these children and others looked after under Section 20 of the Children Act (voluntary accommodation) is known to be a source of confusion. In addition, some authorities may fail to record children as being 'looked after' when they receive short breaks, and thus not include them in the figures.

What is clear, however, is that the focus of most existing short-break provision has been on disabled children and their families. Almost three-quarters of the children recorded in the national statistics as receiving an agreed series of short-term placements did so because of their disability (DoH, 2003). The development of Support Care schemes to support the families of children who are 'in need' for some other reason has been slow, and subject to setbacks. Of four such schemes studied in a research project in the mid

1990s (Aldgate and Bradley, 1999) only one was still operating in 2003. Yet it is unclear why local authorities have been slow to develop this provision. Uncertainty on a number of points could be proving a deterrent. For example, they could be unsure about the legal status of children receiving short breaks. Should they be counted as receiving 'family support' under Section 17 of the Children Act, or 'voluntary accommodation' under Section 20? Have local authorities been put off because they believe that if a child becomes 'looked after' through participation in a Support Care scheme, they would then be required to apply the full benefits (review, care plan, health plan, Personal Education Plan, advocacy and so on), even though the child may only be staying away from home on an infrequent basis?

As part of the *Choice Protects* review, the Thomas Coram Research Unit at London University's Institute of Education was asked to carry out a survey of Support Foster Care schemes, with the aim of finding out more about the nature and extent of this provision. In particular, the study aimed to look at the barriers (legal and otherwise) that might be preventing local authorities from developing this kind of support for families, and how they could be overcome. This chapter provides an overview of some of the main findings of that study, and highlights key issues that local authorities need to consider when developing a Support Foster Care service. The full report has been published by the Institute of Education in collaboration with the Department for Education and Skills (Greenfields and Statham, 2004).

The research study

A short screening questionnaire was sent to all 150 councils with social services responsibilities in England in April 2003, asking whether a Support Foster Care scheme existed or was planned, and about barriers and difficulties that had been experienced or would be anticipated in setting one up. Replies were received from 46 councils, of whom 12 said that they operated a Support Care scheme and 34 that they did not. Some of the latter did offer short breaks on an occasional rather than a structured basis, and there was a definite interest in developing further this form of family support. From the screening survey and other sources, fourteen councils were identified for inclusion in the study: six with an established Support Care scheme, two in the process of setting up such a scheme, and six authorities without a Support Care scheme. They covered a range of local authority types and geographical areas. The schemes themselves varied in scope and size, from those with a single carer and only one child placed so far, to those with a pool of over 20 support carers who supported more than a hundred children a year (see Table 11.1).

Table 11.1 Overview of schemes

LA	Date set up	Location	Support carers	Children placed	Service provided
A	1989	Family Support	7 (+1 being assessed)	Approx 100 per year.	Childminders with dual registration as foster carers, provide short-term support (generally lasting around 3 months) to families with children aged 0–8. May be day care, evenings or overnight stays e.g. 2 days a week or 2 weekends a month. Occasionally short periods of full-time care are offered (max 7 consecutive nights).
B	1996	Family Support	23	142 children placed in 2002/03. Approx 70 families at any one time	Placements tailored to needs of individual family, commonly one weekend a month or 1 or 2 schooldays, especially if child excluded from school. Usually last 6–9 months.
C	1998	Family Support	17	Currently supporting 51 children + 5 introductions + 3 emergency placements.	Flexible service, may be 48-hour block, mid-week or alternate weekends, occasionally provides in-home support e.g. for teenage mother. May be time-limited or longer term and also provides periods of short-term full-time care and emergency placements.
D	1999	Fostering	10	Figures N/A.	Usually 1 weekend a month, with most carers having 2 placements and thus working 2 weekends per month. Mostly 6 months max,

Table 11.1 *Continued*

LA	Date set up	Location	Support carers	Children placed	Service provided
					but 'not set in stone'. Focus on activities with children/young people (e.g. swimming, sports); recreation allowance is provided.
E	1999	Fostering	5 + 3 main-stream who also do short breaks	Approx 7 placements in 2002 and 2003.	Flexibility limited by what carers are able to offer, usually 1 weekend a month. Currently no time limits but may be introduced if scheme expands.
F	1999	Fostering	6 or 7 + 3 main-stream	Approx 8–10 children at any one time	Time-limited service combined with other family support. Typically offers 2 sessions/days a month, for 6 months.
G	2002 (pilot)	Fostering	1 (+4 being assessed)	1 (supported within family)	Developed as respite service for foster carers but hope to extend to support children living at home.
H	2003 (in devt.)	Fostering	None yet	None yet	Plans to develop the service initially on lines of Link service for disabled children, which offers up to 30 days per year.

Information was collected from detailed telephone interviews with co-ordinators of Support Care schemes, senior managers in family placement or fostering teams, and a legal adviser in six authorities. The interviews explored the difficulties experienced in setting up and keeping schemes going, the reasons why local authorities without schemes did not have them, and what had or would prove helpful in overcoming barriers to developing a support foster care service. Managers' views were sought about the factors that facilitate or hinder the use of short-term breaks as a family support service, and the local authority's practice in applying Looked After Children (LAC) procedures to this form of care. Information was also collected on the costs of Support Care schemes compared to mainstream fostering, so far as those who were interviewed were able to provide this. Finally, three of the longer-established schemes were visited, and a group of six or seven foster carers in each took part in a group interview which explored their experiences of offering this kind of care and how and why they had come to do the work. It was not possible within the timescale of the study to talk to parents or children who used the schemes, but information on their views can be found in an earlier study by Aldgate and Bradley (1999) and in Chapter 3 of this book.

Support Care: The philosophy

Support Care schemes shared a number of characteristics and beliefs that distinguished them from mainstream fostering placements. These included:
- Prevention is better than care.
- Parents in control.
- Help in a crisis.
- A flexible response.

Prevention is better than care

A key aim of Support Care was to prevent children needing to be accommodated on a longer-term basis. Schemes had often been set up in response to a perceived lack of support services for families who were struggling to cope, and the hope was that this would avoid the need for more serious intervention later. As one scheme manager explained:

There were a lot of repeat referrals. Families coming in and asking for support, fairly low level stuff but because there weren't any preventative services there, they were being fobbed off; and because they weren't getting any services it was coming back at a far higher level. It might come back in as a child protection matter or children needing to be accommodated.

It was difficult to find solid evidence from the research study to show that providing Support Care did in fact prevent accommodation, since few local authorities kept good enough records of services offered and outcomes for individual children. In particular, it was difficult to prove that children would have entered care had the service not been provided, although the circumstances in which short breaks were offered did demonstrate a high level of need. Anecdotal evidence, including co-ordinators' and carers' views, suggested that short breaks could successfully prevent the need for children to be accommodated longer-term, and the service was highly valued by parents. More formal monitoring and evaluation would be needed, however, to demonstrate the impact on outcomes for children.

Parents in control

An important distinction between Support Care and other forms of accommodation was the emphasis on partnership with parents, and the way in which they were encouraged to take control of their lives during periods of respite from childcare responsibilities. As one scheme manager put it:

What we're trying to do is give parents the message that they have not given up any control, they're the people in the driving seat still with their child. All we're doing is giving them a few breaks to help them to do that. We are not taking over any department of their lives.

The emphasis in Support Care was on strengthening families' own ability to cope with their situation. Sometimes, just knowing that help was available if needed could be a support in itself, even if the service was not taken up. The support carers who provided short breaks offered parents information and advice, told them about local facilities they could use, and provided emotional support and a 'friendly ear' in times of need. They were not generally expected to engage in more formal support for parents, and in most cases seemed to have found ways of negotiating the boundaries of their role and avoiding parents becoming too dependent on them, although this was an area where the availability of support from a scheme manager could be crucial.

Help in a crisis

Most Support Care schemes had a strong philosophy of time-limited acute service delivery, to discourage parental dependence on the service. Short breaks were typically provided for no more than six to nine months, to help parents 'get back on their feet'. There was also an emphasis on Support Care as part of a package of support to enable the family to overcome temporary difficulties. This could be work with parents (such as support by social workers or family support workers) or other services for children (such as attendance at a child and adolescent mental health clinic). One scheme co-ordinator explained that 'these things only work if social workers are using the 'feel good' effect to get in and do a piece of work'.

A flexible response

Although the schemes included in our study varied considerably in size and scope, all were able to offer a flexible response depending on families' needs. This most commonly involved providing a weekend break every fortnight or month, but could also involve care in the daytime (for younger children or those excluded from school), overnight stays during the week, or short periods of full-time care. A good example of the latter was when two young children whose mother had severe mental health problems were provided with short breaks on a regular basis, and were also placed full-time with the same trusted carer when their mother needed to be admitted to hospital.

The flexibility of Support Care schemes was also illustrated in the plans some scheme co-ordinators outlined for how their projects could potentially be developed in the future. These included:

- Greater support for 'friends and family' carers.
- Links to remand fostering schemes.
- Working with young runaways.
- Working with children excluded from school.
- A 'buddying' scheme for young people at risk of social exclusion, including care leavers and teenage parents.
- Post-adoption support.
- Carers being trained to facilitate family group conferences.

Support Care: The costs

It was difficult to obtain full financial information on the costs of setting up and running a Support Care scheme in some local authorities, especially when funds were not separately allocated within fostering service budgets. Generally, payments made to carers were very low, often at or below the lowest rate of payment made to full-time foster carers. In one local authority, a 'weekend recreational allowance' was paid on top of a small fee to encourage carers to take children on outings and to leisure facilities, and two other schemes offered their support carers a small retainer fee in recognition of the intermittent nature of the work. Unsurprisingly, the low pay was a source of discontent for some carers, especially those who had prior mainstream fostering experience. They felt that it did not reflect the demanding nature of the work and was an indication that their service was seen as less important by the local authority than that provided by full-time foster carers.

Based upon the limited data most interviewees were able to supply on the costs of schemes, Support Care did appear to be significantly less costly than providing care for accommodated children. This was partly because of the much shorter time that children were looked after away from home. One co-ordinator noted that 'to place a child in Support Care for a weekend once a month for a year' would cost the same as one week in an external placement'. The direct costs (retainers and fees) of providing a family with the Support Care service in this authority averaged £550 per child, although the length of individual placements varied considerably. Another co-ordinator calculated that the whole Support Care budget, including her salary, was less than the cost of a family of three in an out-of-county placement for a year.

Several managers described Support Care as 'investing to save', and argued that it must be cost effective compared to the costs of full-time accommodation for children. This argument depends, of course, on establishing that short breaks can indeed prevent the need for expensive full-time accommodation, which has yet to be clearly demonstrated. However, the costs of providing a dedicated Support Care scheme (between £200,000 and £250,000 a year to cover the salaries of a scheme manager, one or two support workers, an administrator and payments to carers, according to figures provided by two of the better established schemes in the study) appear reasonably low when considering the number of children and families who were able to benefit from the service.

Barriers to developing a Support Care service

In both the survey and the interviews with local authority officers, the barriers that might be preventing local authorities from developing Support Care schemes were explored.

Recruiting foster carers

The issue raised most often by local authority managers responding to the survey was the difficulty many local authorities were experiencing in finding and keeping carers for mainstream (full-time) fostering. Those without schemes feared that similar difficulties would apply to Support Care, or even that the pool of potential foster carers would be further diminished by the development of short-break services. In practice, finding carers to work in a Support Care scheme had not proved particularly difficult, with co-ordinators of schemes reporting that they had targeted carers with a different profile from mainstream foster care. Often these were people who had 'wanted to foster for a long time' but who were not eligible for mainstream fostering as they worked on a full-time basis, or had age or health issues which precluded them from taking up full-time fostering.

Support Care also appeared to offer a route into fostering for individuals who were attracted to the idea of caring work, but at the current time only wished to 'dip a toe in the water'. In a number of authorities, co-ordinators reported that support carers had moved into mainstream fostering once they had experience of working for the service. A further group of carers (found in the majority of authorities) consisted of former full-time foster carers who were disillusioned with mainstream caring work, or felt that they had reached an age where they wished to cut back on their commitment to the service, or sought a more varied role. Two authorities reported that they had recruited support carers from amongst the adult children of mainstream foster carers. Rather than providing competition for a scarce resource, it seemed that Support Care schemes could actually draw in people who might later move on to offer full-time care, as well as keeping other foster carers within the service.

Lack of priority to preventive services

Resource issues (staffing, payment and funding) were mentioned in both the survey and the interviews as a significant barrier to the development of a support foster care service. Local authorities with schemes had often struggled to develop them due to funding constraints, and managers in authorities without schemes generally thought that it would be difficult to allocate money to such preventive work, even though they might personally favour doing so. The following comment was fairly typical:

Preventive work has taken a bit of a hammering. The focus is on areas with performance indicators, and it's difficult to demonstrate that preventive work reduces the number of looked after children.

Until resource issues are fully addressed, the development of Support Care schemes is likely to remain hampered by low staffing levels, the need to bid for funds on an annual basis, staff insecurity, difficulties in capacity building and forward planning, and a potential drain of carers to more lucrative forms of employment.

The legal status of children receiving Support Care

Legal issues, such as whether children receiving Support Care needed to be treated as looked after under Section 20 of the Children Act, were rarely mentioned as a barrier to setting up schemes, but they did become more of an issue once schemes were operating. There was widespread confusion and varying practice with regard to the need for reviews, medicals and care plans for children receiving Support Care. Most schemes had decided to operate some form of 'slimmed down' looked After Children procedures, but were unsure of the legality of this. All authorities reported that they would welcome clarification and guidance from the Government in this area.

Where should a Support Care service be based?

Although the majority of schemes in the study were located within family placement or fostering and adoption teams, several had moved to a base within family support services. The nature of Support Care is distinct from mainstream fostering (a point made by both co-ordinators and carers) and support carers and staff often felt as though they did not fit comfortably into fostering services. They reported that some families could feel stigmatised by the location of the service (as well as the need for children to become looked after), and disempowered by the project's association with fostering. Most co-ordinators had tried to address such concerns by referring to their scheme as 'family support', or avoiding the use of headed paper containing terms such as fostering or adoption. The ideal for many was some kind of hybrid status, whereby the scheme was located and seen to be somewhere between fostering and family support.

This was partly because there were also advantages if support carers had strong links with family placement services. These included easier access to the training and support offered to mainstream foster carers, and the possibility of offering families a flexible service combining short breaks with longer periods of accommodation if support carers were also registered to provide short-term care. The key message appeared to be the importance of developing close links between family placement and family support services and ensuring that Support Care is presented to families in an accessible, non-stigmatising way, regardless of where the service is actually based.

Messages for planners

The findings from this study suggest a number of areas that local authorities need to consider when developing Support Care services.

Strategic planning

When Support Care schemes have been developed in an isolated way, rather than as part of an integrated policy on services for children and families, they are particularly vulnerable to budget cuts and marginalisation. Such projects had often continued only because of the commitment and determination of staff and carers, and others had failed when a particular manager or co-ordinator left their post or short-term funding ended. Financial support through the *Choice Protects* initiative has been welcomed by local authorities and has had a significant impact on the development of Support Care in many areas. Partnerships with other agencies (such as with Health and Sure Start in one authority) have also provided additional income to enable projects to expand. However, insecurity over the fate of schemes once short-term funding ends highlights the need for projects to be incorporated into mainstream budgets (either family support or fostering) wherever possible.

An integrated strategy, where Support Care has a clear role within the range of council services for children, would help to ensure that preventive services like this do not lose out when decisions are being made about resource allocation. Such a strategy would also need to take a co-ordinated view of how services offered by different agencies to support families fit together, for example the relationship between the daycare purchased by local authorities for children in need from community or 'sponsored' childminders, and the care provided by short-break foster carers.

Legal requirements

Although the majority of Support Care schemes currently look after children under Section 20 of the Children Act, and register those providing short-break care as foster carers, there is considerable variation in how the various regulatory requirements are interpreted and amended by local authorities to achieve a better 'fit' with the nature of Support Care. Further clarification is expected from central government but, in the meantime, local authority legal departments may be able to provide those wishing to set up a scheme with advice on how best to modify Looked After Children documentation and procedures to make them less unwieldy and more appropriate to the provision of short-break care. Issues raised by legal officers are discussed further in the full report of the research study (Greenfields and Statham, 2004).

Support and training for carers

Focus group discussions with carers highlighted the importance of offering a good support package to carers, who form the backbone of any scheme. They would welcome similar support to that enjoyed by mainstream foster carers, such as carers' group meetings, access to equipment, 24-hour 'on-call' advice and regular supervision. Such support could be offered by dedicated workers attached to schemes, or possibly by embedding the support carers into the fostering service so that each fostering team member has some support carers on their workload, as happened in one authority in our study. When co-ordinators were running schemes single-handed, it was generally difficult for them to provide the support and supervision that carers needed.

The good relationships which scheme co-ordinators had been able to establish with their support carers were repeatedly mentioned as a crucial factor in the success of the service, and it is important that they are able to allocate sufficient time to this.

Training for support carers needs to involve a mixture of weekend and evening sessions to ensure that employed carers are able to attend without loss of earnings or having to use annual leave entitlement. Whilst most local authorities who offer Support Care currently ensure their carers complete the same pre-registration training as mainstream foster carers, there are arguments in favour of offering a shortened form of training, devised on an in-house basis by Support Care co-ordinators and managers, and focusing on issues of particular relevance to Support Care such as working with parents. Two authorities in our study had also created opportunities for support carers to expand their role, for example by running support groups for parents of children with behavioural difficulties, or acting as facilitators for family group conferences.

Pay and allowances

Although financial reward was not the primary motivation for undertaking Support Care work, issues around pay and allowances were a source of considerable dissatisfaction to many carers. They expressed concerns about the rate of pay, which in most cases was extremely low; inconsistencies between carers within the same scheme; late payments; the expectation that they would provide activities for children placed with them out of their own pockets; and lack of access to resources that were available to mainstream foster carers such as loyalty bonuses, clothing allowances and computers. They were often left feeling that their work was not valued or adequately rewarded by the local authority. Issues such as these need to be addressed when schemes are being set up, and decisions made about whether support carers are to be paid on a fostering scale (and where on the scale they should be placed) or on a specific Support Care rate which reflects the parental support element of their work.

Good communication between teams and with carers

The study suggests that clearer lines of communication need to be established between various social work teams. Social workers sometimes had unrealistic expectations of what Support Care schemes could offer, expecting them to act as a source of emergency placements or failing to provide adequate information about the level of a child's needs. Some carers reported that they were increasingly being asked to care for children with quite severe behavioural or psychological difficulties when they were neither trained nor equipped to deal with this. The issue of placements for children with Attention Deficit Hyperactivity Disorder (ADHD) or who were on the autistic spectrum was a major point of discussion in all three focus groups. Carers referred to the changing emphasis of their caring role, from providing support to families under stress to providing respite for parents whose children were on the verge of accommodation because of disabilities and behavioural difficulties. Whilst carers accepted that children receiving the service often had more complex needs than when the service was initiated, they were often dissatisfied with the lack of communication and support they received from social workers. Scheme co-ordinators could perform a valuable role in such circumstances by acting as a buffer or bridge between social worker and support carer.

Better record keeping

Few Support Care schemes collected systematic information about the children who are cared for, including records of previous or subsequent contact with social services, and outcomes for children and their families. Collecting and analysing such data would enable schemes to demonstrate the impact of their service on children and families, and needs to be considered when services are being established.

Conclusion

This chapter reports on a research project that investigated the nature and extent of Support Care schemes in England, and explored the barriers that might be preventing local authorities from developing this service for children in need. The study revealed a complex picture: a small number of local authorities have developed specialist schemes to provide short breaks for children and support for their parents, whilst others are offering this service on an occasional basis using mainstream foster carers. At the same time, some community childminding networks are exploring the potential to offer a similar service (including overnight care), but under different regulations. The legal requirements for placing children in this form of care are unclear, and clarification is needed on the issues involved, in particular whether Support Care needs to be provided under Section 20 of the Children Act or whether it can be offered as a form of family support under Section 17. The research suggests that there is a need for a more integrated approach to providing this kind of support to families, both at a local authority level (locating Support Care firmly within a spectrum of services to children and families) and at national level (for example, greater dialogue between the regulatory bodies responsible for childminding and for foster care).

Support Care schemes do appear able to offer a particularly flexible response to the needs of families in times of stress, and to help children to remain cared for at home. The commitment of the scheme co-ordinators and support carers to providing this service was evident throughout the study, often in difficult circumstances and for very little financial reward. In the words of one social services senior manager, 'it's a small resource which goes a long way'. The increasing attention being given to developing such provision, and monitoring its impact, means that it should be possible before long to demonstrate that Support Care may indeed be an example of 'investing to save'.

References

Aldgate, J. and Bradley, M. (1999) *Supporting Families through Short-term Fostering*. London: The Stationery Office.

Audit Commission (2003) *Services for Disabled Children: a Review of Services for Disabled Children and their Families*. London: Audit Commission.

DoH (2003) *Children Looked After by Local Authorities: Statistics for the Year Ending 31 March 2002, England*. London: DoH.

DoH (2002) *Choice Protects: Update Bulletin No. 1*. www.doh.gov.uk/ choiceprotects

DoH (1995) *Child Protection: Messages from Research*. London: HMSO.

Greenfields, M. and Statham, J. (2004) *Support Foster Care: Developing a Short-break Service for Children in Need. Understanding Children's Social Care Series No. 8*. London: Institute of Education, London University.

HM Treasury (2003) *Every Child Matters*. (CM5860). London: The Stationery Office.

Tarleton, B. (2002) *Better for the Break: Short Breaks for Children with Autistic Disorders and their Families*. Bristol: Norah Fry Research Centre, University of Bristol.

Quinton, D. (2004) *Supporting Parents: Messages from Research*. London: Jessica Kingsley.